The Glory
to Glory
SISTERHOOD

The Glory
to Glory
SISTERHOOD

God's Sorority

Robin Kirby-Gatto

Previously published as God's Sorority 2007 by Tate Publishing & Enterprises, LLC
ISBN 978-1-60247-732-2

DESTINY IMAGE® PUBLISHERS, INC.

P.O. Box 310, Shippensburg, PA 17257-0310

"Speaking to the Purposes of God for This Generation and for the Generations to Come."

This book and all other Destiny Image, Revival Press, MercyPlace, Fresh Bread, Destiny Image Fiction, and Treasure House books are available at Christian bookstores and distributors worldwide.

For a U.S. bookstore nearest you, call 1-800-722-6774.

For more information on foreign distributors, call 717-532-3040.

Reach us on the Internet: www.destinyimage.com.

Trade Paper ISBN 13: 978-0-7684-3238-1
Hard Cover ISBN 13: 978-0-7684-3430-9
Large Print ISBN 13: 978-0-7684-3431-6
Ebook ISBN 13: 978-0-7684-9059-6

For Worldwide Distribution, Printed in the U.S.A.
1 2 3 4 5 6 7 8 9 10 11 / 13 12 11 10

Dedication

I dedicate this book, *The Glory to Glory Sisterhood*, to you. You, woman of God, are a Holy Nation and a Royal Priesthood. You are a woman who has been created to bring the Kingdom of Heaven to earth. You are a woman who has greatness inside of her. You are a woman who walks in the divine plans and purposes of God. You are a woman who serves King Jesus, without regard to the reproach you might have to bear for your devotion. You are a woman after God's heart!

I love you! Robin

Acknowledgments

I want to acknowledge God the Father, Jesus Christ, and the Holy Ghost for allowing me to be the instrument of Glory to Glory Sisterhood. I want to thank my husband, Richard Gatto—without his love, support, and encouragement, I would not be the woman that I am now. I thank you for never allowing me to give up on this dream and for being the biggest dream-chaser of anyone I know. You are my lover, my confidant, and my best friend. I thank God that He gave you to me on this side of Heaven, and I look forward to seeing you fully in the glory of God when we go home.

I want to thank my children, Christopher and Matthew Kirby, for their patience and support while I wrote as well as bringing me much joy in life. I want to thank Sheila Guidry for praying and encouraging me through the process, and for her invaluable mentorship when I was under her. I also want to thank my mom and dad, David and Rebecca Ward, for loving me through life and raising me in the House of God, as well as for staying on your knees and praying for me during the hard times. I want to thank my sister, Liz Anne Elsea, for being a sister in Christ and praying for me, and also for being an awesome little sister. Thanks to my brother, David, for his tender heart. Also, thanks to all the Princess Warriors—Sheila, Pam, Suzy, Sonya, Holly, Beth, Sue, and Brandi—for all their prayers over this book. I want to thank Pastor Mark Sims for believing in this book and encouraging me, and thanks to all my friends and church family at Kingwood Church.

I would also like to acknowledge Don Milam and thank him for taking on this project, *The Glory to Glory Sisterhood,* and for being a coach for authors to bring out the best in them. I never would have added the other sections had you not encouraged me and known it was in me. I would like to thank Tracy Shuman with Destiny Image for her time and efforts in this project. Finally, thanks to Destiny Image for taking on this project—you have made my God-dreams tangible and visible. God bless you!

Contents

Foreword

As a woman who has a great love for the Lord and a strong desire to be like Christ, I have struggled and still struggle with some things in my life that keep me from moving forward in my walk toward freedom in Christ. Having read all four books of *The Glory to Glory Sisterhood* series, these words are strongly inbred in me now—"deliverance," "understanding," "compassion," "zeal," and "warrior."

Each book stands on its own in giving valuable insight to your faith walk. This first book is an inspiriting stepping-stone that leads you into each book that follows, making you feel as though you are moving from glory to glory with each one. You can feel Robin guided by the Holy Spirit on each page of this series. *The Glory to Glory Sisterhood* has not only helped me realize that the Word is my sword against all those things holding me back in life, but it has also given me the exact words to use as weapons against those attacks. There were great revelations through these books, not just on how I should look and feel toward my sisters in Christ, but also on how to be the wife I am meant to be. Most importantly, it gave me revelation on what type of daughter I am meant to be for my Heavenly Father.

This series is not only for those who are seeking God and Jesus Christ as their Savior, but it's also for those who have long since accepted Christ and already know the Bible. Every woman following God will be greatly blessed by reading this series. I can now say, after reading *The Glory to Glory Sisterhood*, I am a princess warrior for the Most High God, and I pray daily for my sisters in Christ to be raised to a higher glory through Christ our Savior.

Liz Anne Elsea

Preface

Sitting down to write a book on God's sorority was intimidating to say the least. First, it is far out there and stretches my comfort zone. I realize that some people might be offended at the concept of God having a sorority. However, He has given me confirmation after confirmation.

God's heartbeat is to destroy the walls of prejudice, conspiracy, and suspicion that have been built up between women. It is His desire that, when different women see each other walking through the mall, on the street, in the market, and throughout the world, they would look at each other and respond, "My sister." If we are truly born into the Kingdom of God and have His Holy Spirit in us, we will have this seed of sisterhood inside of us.

> *How good and pleasant it is when brothers [sisters] live together in unity! It is like precious oil poured on the head, running down on the beard, running down on Aaron's beard, down upon the collar of his robes. It is as if the dew of Hermon were falling on Mount Zion. For there the Lord bestows His blessing, even life forevermore (Psalm 133:1-3 NIV).*

*May the God who gives endurance and encouragement give you
a spirit of unity among yourselves as you follow Christ Jesus, so
that with one heart and mouth you may glorify the God and
Father of our Lord Jesus Christ* (Romans 15:5-6 NIV).

I would like to preface this book with the fact that God desires to bring down walls separating women in all cultures, age groups, and social groups. His heart beats for His daughters to be united in Him.

*Be completely humble and gentle; be patient, bearing with
one another in love. Make every effort to keep the unity of the
Spirit through the bond of peace. There is one body and one
Spirit—just as you were called to one hope when you were
called* (Ephesians 4:2-4 NIV).

God loves for His daughters to have unity. Unity means being one. As we see in the United States, the 50 states joined together as one under a common union to create a nation that would live in harmony and peace, protecting the people of the entire nation. Likewise, girls, young women, middle-aged women, and older women have a makeup different from each other, involving different socioeconomics, cultures, languages, trends, and so on. However, we are created to come together in unity under one God, one King, with one Holy Spirit. Together, this unity of the female gender is "God's Sorority." His sorority is the "Glory to Glory Sisterhood," taken from the Scripture in Second Corinthians:

*But we all, with unveiled face, beholding as in a mirror
the glory of the Lord, are being transformed into the same
image from glory to glory, just as by the Spirit of the Lord*
(2 Corinthians 3:18).

Join in the greatest sorority ever to dwell on earth, and come into a life of newness where your sisters eagerly await your entrance into the Glory to Glory Sisterhood!

Introduction

This first book of *The Glory to Glory Sisterhood* series establishes the cornerstone—Jesus Christ in us, the Hope of Glory. First, we find out who we are as individuals before we come together corporately. It is our very own individualism—our testimony, the things we have overcome—that add to the sisterhood as a whole. Then we will understand how sisters are to treat each other—by looking at what we should do and should not do in the sisterhood. Next, we will look upon Jesus, the gateway into the Glory to Glory Sisterhood. We will gaze into the eyes of Jesus and see the very heartbeat He has for His beautiful princesses. Finally, we will take a look at the glory of God and what we can expect to see with His glory in our lives.

The other three books deal with the fear of the Lord, spiritual warfare, forgiveness, rejection, jealousy, deliverance from sin, hearing God, and destiny. After reading the entire series, each woman should be able to turn around and be "big sisters" in the sisterhood, mentoring other women.

Shortly before finalizing this book, God stretched me further when He told me that He wanted me to write a Glory to Glory Sisterhood rap song. This was too much for me, and I asked Him for confirmation. All through my head for weeks, I kept hearing the "Rapper's Delight" song by the Sugarhill Gang, which I used to roller skate to when I was younger. Then, after asking God for a movie to watch, He led me to one with a kangaroo in it. Shortly into the movie, the kangaroo started singing "Rapper's Delight." I realized if God could use a talking donkey to get His word out to stop a corrupt prophet, He could use a singing kangaroo to give me confirmation.

GLORY TO GLORY SISTERHOOD RAP SONG

There is a new sisterhood coming up the pike,
and we are united under Messiah Jesus Christ.

He came to shed His blood so we could be free,
which is why we have silver—it stands for redeemed.

We're coming to ya with fuchsia, which stands for chaste,
because we want to be glorious when we see Him face to face.

And finally, there's the color black for humility;
that's where it's at.

Oh Hallelujah! We've come to bring Heaven down.
And that's why the Glory to Glory Sisterhood
is coming to your town!

I said "Ho-ho-hum-hum," we've got a race we've come to run.
We will not stop or give in until we reach the end!

We raise our hands and praise the King
and like Miriam we shake tambourine.

Princess warriors like Jael, God trains our hands to war.

*For His Kingdom suffers violence and
the violent take it by force.*

Tell me women do you have the mind of Christ? ("Yes!")

*Our weapons of warfare are not carnal,
pulling down the enemy's lies.*

*Our God is bigger and stronger than the enemy.
And that is why we say the name Jesus
to that everything bows its knee.*

*I said a "Ho-ho-ha-ha," we will fight
with worship and praise.
God will raise a standard and scatter
the enemy in seven ways.*

*Holy is our Lord and worthy to be praised.
He is the God of power and love and mercy is His way.*

*Tell me women do you pursue holiness? ("Yes!")
Are you consecrated to God like a Zadok priestess? ("Yes!")*

*Like Ezekiel we watch the Lord's gates;
we love what He loves and we hate what He hates.*

*We confess that we are vessels as Romans 9:23.
We are mercy vessels created for the Lord's glory!*

We are the Glory to Glory Sisterhood!

There Is Always
a Story; What
Is Yours?

SECTION ONE

Many of us have a "story" of what God has brought us through in our lives. It is our story—that is, a testimony for others to hear how God has helped us overcome in every circumstance and trial. The Word of God says we overcome by the Blood of the Lamb and the word of testimony (see Rev. 12:11).

c h a p t e r

1

Robin's Story

Going into my freshman year of college, I believed somewhere in the crevices of my heart that I wanted to be part of a sorority. It is somewhat of a tradition in the South for a young lady to join a sorority, although few actually do. In sorority rush, there is a "legacy." This is where the daughter of an alumnus to a sorority seeks admittance, and her legacy makes it almost certain that she will be accepted.

In high school, I had been one who moved in different groups; I didn't like cliques and had no desire to be a part of one. This was different. Why was it that I, someone who had been so independent, now desired to be in a sisterhood in college? A part of me liked being separated from such organizations, because I had seen that at times they excluded others—a trait I loathed. In addition, I didn't like their rules and regulations, because they implied that maintaining membership was conditional upon behaviors or performance. It appeared that their care was not genuine, but conditional.

Unbreakable Bonds

This book is about being a part of a sisterhood that is deep and is founded on unbreakable bonds. It is my belief that all women deeply desire to be in such a sisterhood. We travel many pathways through our lives—paths that indicate both the desire to belong to a sisterhood and the desire to be separate. In the threads of my story, you can see times in my life when satan and his demons tried to make me feel unaccepted, rejected, unloved, unwanted, and like a "bad girl." The enemy uses these tactics to make us feel separated from God. However, it is God's desire for us to be separated from the world. This is a story to help others and bring freedom to the female gender individually and corporately.

High School

For most of my high school life, I was a very independent person. As a strong practicing Christian for the majority of my high school years, I walked a different path from most girls. I was one who detested any group of girls that made fun of or did not accept the "nerdy girls." I hung out with these "nerdy girls" much of the time and enjoyed watching them being pulled out of their shell. It was my desire for them to feel special. I was a cheerleader and the baseball statistician for the boy's baseball team; I was labeled "wittiest" of the school and "best dressed," and I was voted to homecoming court twice. I was not considered a "nerdy girl."

However, God had given me such compassion for those "left out" that I desired to be around them instead of those that were "accepted." Sometimes, I would stand up to the bully of the bus stop when I was tired of watching him be mean to others. One day when I was around 14 or 15 years old, he actually picked me up over his head and threw me to the ground. Immediately, I jumped back up and told him that I didn't care how many times he was going to throw me down or hurt me, because I was still going to get back up and get in his face. I was brave, spunky, a fighter for those who didn't fight, almost fearless. This was not a picture of someone who needed or desired to be part of some young women's group in a college sorority. So what happened? I was one who stood out and wanted to be with those who were not accepted into sororities. When did I change?

Young Love Breakup

At the end of my junior year of high school, I started dating a young man who was thought of as the "popular guy" at school. I was smitten with him. We were in a serious dating relationship, and I thought he was the person for me. It seemed to be a perfect relationship.

I had been in another serious relationship during my first year in high school as well. He had dumped me for a girl who would be intimate with him, and as a freshman, I had gone to God with my hurt. I then went through a transitional period, but not to the same extent as the one in my junior year. When my relationship as a junior ended, I did not take my hurt to God.

The popular guy I dated in my junior year dumped me for another popular girl, one that was more popular and older than I was. I was devastated beyond measure. At this point, things began changing, and this was where bondages began to establish themselves in my life.

I had come to a crossroads where I would choose my path. One path was to take my hurt to God the Father and let Him heal me, as I had done after my first breakup. The other path was to deal with the hurt on my own and heal it myself. I chose the latter and turned to alcohol and inappropriate behaviors. I was angry and determined that I would not let another guy hurt me and, even more than that, would not let someone reject me again.

Rejection

Little did I know that this spirit of rejection would revisit me throughout much of my adulthood. Young and considered attractive, I had many suitors who desired to go out with me. However, I had changed and was no longer a sweet, fearless, independent young lady; I had become dependent on being accepted by others. Earlier, I had been strictly dependent on God. Now, since

I had turned to people for acceptance, I was set up for disappointment, broken relationships, and unhealed wounds.

I turned to a life of partying, which led to bad decisions and unbecoming behavior, especially for a Christian. I became the life of the party, was accepted among my peers (the popular ones), and started gravitating toward the group of people that tended to not accept others. Little did I know that this would take me down a road to a place where I was losing my identity and my purpose in life. Guys I would have never considered before became my choice for dating.

By my senior year, drinking had become part of my life. All of this behavior stemmed from my breakup the year before. I had allowed a small and insignificant breakup to be magnified more than it should have. Moreover, I listened to the lies of the enemy and came into agreement with oaths that I should have never made, for they were not of God. I promised myself that I "would never let another guy hurt me." It was my determination to become indifferent with a guy at even the smallest indication that he was about to reject me.

I had built up a wall of rejection with men, and I found myself caring about things I had never cared for much. On the other hand, things that I used to consider important I was becoming indifferent toward—for example, hanging out with the "nerdy girls." We had so many great slumber parties and nights together. They were real with me, and I truly enjoyed their company. However, as I began changing in my senior year of high school, I found myself desiring to hang around the popular girls. Somehow, I was spending less time with the other girls, neglecting the purpose in my life at that time.

REBELLION

I had even become rebellious toward my parents, and it was not "hormones" like much of Western culture believes. Personally, I believe accepting rebellious behavior from teens and discounting it as hormones does them a disservice and enables unacceptable behaviors. Because I had been hurt earlier in my life and I was not allowing God to heal me, I was left trying to heal myself through making a "change." How many times have we said that growing up? "I'm going to make a change."

The reason I was now changing was that I had begun to experience the enemy's attack on my life. I allowed the spirit of rejection to cause me to feel unwanted, unloved, and unaccepted. Because of my rejection, I became more aggressive in all areas of my life. This created behaviors that would cause others to reject me and established a cycle. My behaviors caused others to reject me, which made me feel like a "bad girl." This is very important because this is how satan's lie builds upon each event in life. The enemy wants us to believe that we are bad because God the Father created His daughters to feel like they are princesses and "good girls." Everything that God creates is "good," and we are to do "good works" (see Gen. 1:31; Eph. 2:10 NIV). The enemy wants us to feel the opposite—that we are "bad."

God the Father placed in the female gender the innate ability—demonstrated through the mother–child relationship—to love and nurture those around us. Thus, as created vessels of nurturing, our emotional language makes us expect to be nurtured as well. However, the enemy sets it up so that the contrary happens. Then, when we get into a situation where we are rejected, we almost feel like we were hit in the face with a frying pan. Instead of receiving nurturing, we get a mighty blow on the cheek with that frying pan and exclaim, "Oh, that hurt!" The father of lies agrees with the pain and tells us that the reason is because we were bad girls. Satan wants us to agree that we are bad girls. This is exactly what I had done. I had come into agreement with the belief that I was a bad girl when I acted in an unbecoming fashion to others, and they did not accept me as a result. Rejection was painful, and I now wanted to be nurtured and accepted.

PARTY TIME

College started, and I was attending a university that was known for its partying—a fact that I actually bragged about. I applied for sorority rush and went through the process to see if I would be accepted by a sorority. If I was, would it be one that I would accept in return? Even among the sororities and fraternities, there were still those organizations that people didn't want to be a part of because of their undesirable reputation. These were "nerdy sororities," so to speak. (This is not to be offensive to any fraternal organization, but rather to speak the truth, because until we do, we cover it up and believe a lie. This book is about confronting the enemy and exposing the lies.)

Rush week—a process of finding a sorority and being accepted by one—was a thrill for me. I went to the different sorority parties and was either invited back the next day or not invited back. I was also crossing out sororities that I didn't want to join. This continued until I ended up making my top two choices, and although we were supposed to put three, I got my first pick. I was excited and felt accepted to say the least, unlike other girls who either didn't get their first or second pick or who couldn't get accepted into any sorority.

During that first year, my partying lifestyle was acceptable to the sorority, and I was actually encouraged in my drinking at times. I amazed people with my capacity to hold so much alcohol and "drink people under the table." I felt accepted—like a mascot, so to speak. I remember going to parties and hanging out with the president and the seniors. They were so much fun and really seemed to accept me as I was.

BLACKBALLED

However, in my second year, things changed. A Christian became president, and my behavior was, of course, unacceptable at that time. The leadership attempted to work with me and put me on probation. During this time, I was a little sister of a fraternity in which the same thing was occurring. I had been accepted as little sister into a fraternity that knew of my partying lifestyle.

After the change in the presidencies of the sorority and fraternity, my drinking problem continued—now I was going against the rules. As a result of my undesired behavior, I was "blackballed" from the sorority and from being a little sister of the fraternity. My grades at the end of the first semester of my sophomore year in college were a joke, and I was, too. I didn't value myself, and neither did anyone else. I do not blame the sorority or fraternity, because they really didn't know what to do with me.

CROSSROADS

I was publicly rejected in front of the masses. There were no secrets when such unpleasant things happened in the sororities or among the little sisters of fraternities. Everyone knew that I had been kicked out, and most of my horrendous behaviors and alcohol problems were common knowledge as well. My rebellion brought me to another crossroads, though I truly did not see it. At that point, I could go to the Father and let Him heal me, or I could heal myself through devices, bad choices, and bad relationships. Again, I chose the latter.

I spun into a series of bad choices that lasted until later on in life (when I finally came to know the Father and His love for me). When I was 19 years old, I married a young man for a brief period of nine months and was severely abused in that relationship—starved, beaten, locked in a house for a few days, and so much more. After that marriage ended, I dwindled to 87 pounds and was insecure and confused, and my mind was so dysfunctional that I was a basket case. It took several years for me to recuperate from this short marriage and the evil strongholds that it brought into my life.

c h a p t e r

2

Robin's "Overcoming" Testimony

I did go on to marry again when I was 21 in 1990, to a young man in medical school. During that marriage, I received my bachelor's degree in social work. I had positions during my schooling where I worked with abused children, the mentally ill, and the elderly.

I was with my husband through his four years of medical school and involved on the medical spouse's auxiliary board. My life became enmeshed with his dreams because I also sought to do medical social work with the elderly. Then, when he had finished medical school and received his MD, we went on to look for a place where he could practice his residency as a doctor. My parents lived in Birmingham, Alabama, and we looked for a program there in order to be closer to them. We moved from Jackson, Mississippi, to Birmingham, into a nice home in the area and by that time had a two-year-old son, Christopher. I continued to work in social work with the elderly, and then we had a second son, Matthew. At that point, I had determined to quit work in order to pursue my master's degree in social work.

Then, in my first semester of master's classes in 1997, my husband left me with one- and six-year-old boys and married another young woman. I went on to receive my master's degree in social work and worked in outpatient psychiatry and home health.

DIVORCE A SURPRISE

I could not see the divorce coming. However, God was so awesome because He had me attending the master's program at the University of Alabama right before my husband left me.

One of the staff members was like a father figure to me, and I felt comfortable telling him about the behavior of my husband. I remember distinctly one time when I came to him and told him of my husband's behavior, and the staff member looked at me and said, "Robin, your husband is fixing to leave you." I was shocked! I was stunned! I could not believe what I was hearing. The very next week, it happened. It was almost as if I was blind.

I was standing in our dining room the day that my husband told me he was leaving me. He just simply said that he did not love me any longer and was leaving. I could not compute the fact that the man I had been married to did not love me. Because of the shock, I never thought for a second that it was because of another woman. I simply was too shocked and still computing in my mind that he did not love me.

However, after awhile, God led a couple of doctors to tell their wives to call me and tell me that my husband was having an affair with a younger woman he worked with. When they told me the woman's name, I was furious because I remembered him talking about her. I thought she was maybe 17; however, I found out later that she was a couple of years older than that and had pursued my husband. I called her at her work and told her to stop seeing him, but she refused. She said my husband did not love me anymore.

Finally, I received peace from the Lord toward the woman, with whom my husband was now living. I told her two things: I could choose to hate her and want to beat her up—or I could forgive her. I then stated to her, "I'm going to forgive you." However, with that being said, I told her one last thing: "I will be fine and move on eventually, but what you have to live with is the fact that my two boys' father is no longer around, and you have a part in that."

I then had peace from God in allowing myself to release her from the offenses she had committed against me and my boys.

Divorce Support Group

I remember the first nine months of the divorce doing nothing but seeking God. I did not go out nor drink because all I wanted was to be with the Lord.

Having been in social work, I knew that I was in need of help. I found a divorce support group to get involved with at a local church on Sundays and took the boys to church there, too. That divorce support group then led me to meeting new friends. Those friends then led me to another group that met during the week as additional support. I joined that group and started hanging around a couple of ladies that drink on occasion. I joined them for one of those occasions and had something to drink. That one occasion unfortunately was all it took to get me addicted to alcohol again because of my past history. I started drinking at home and would rarely go out. However, as a result of my poor choice in drinking I made some bad decisions and became promiscuous again. I stopped seeking the Lord and started feeding my pain with alcohol. I would binge drink a lot during that time.

Suicidal Struggle

It was during this time as I was going to the divorce support group and attending school, that I became suicidal. I felt as though "I did not matter." It is hard to describe this even now. The pain of my divorce with the doctor literally ripped my soul, my heart. We were married for a little over seven years and I had made him my idol; I worshiped him. As a result, when he left me I discovered that my whole world had been built around him and had crumbled to the ground. The pain, plus the lies of the enemy telling me that I did not matter, all built up to distort my perception. I did not desire to be alive anymore and I was so overwhelmed with my life that I just wanted to give up and die. I could not bare being alive. The rejection of the divorce had stirred up the wound of the prior rejections I had experienced and I felt as though I was a huge failure in life.

LIFE AGAIN!

During the time that I was married to the doctor and then as a single mother, I continued to keep my boys in church. I had grown up in church, and as a result of my heritage of being in church I wanted my boys to receive the same benefit. Therefore, I had attended a few churches during this period of my pain. Finally, God had planned for me to go to Kingwood. The way He planned it was so funny.

At that time I had a car tag that had "BELEVER" on the back for the word "believer." It was not to denote that I was a Christian but the popular phrase of "believing in yourself." I went to a gas station to get a six-pack of beer, and as I was getting the beer, one of the ministry students from the program at Kingwood came to me and said, "Ma'am I don't think you should be drinking that beer with that car tag." He thought that I had "BELEVER" because I was a Christian. Immediately, I looked at him and said, "Jesus came to save the world and not to condemn it. Instead of telling me that I shouldn't be drinking this beer why don't you ask me why I'm drinking this beer? Have you walked in my footsteps; do you know what I'm feeling?"

Needless to say, the young student realized he had said the wrong thing, and a third-year ministry school student came up and ministered to me. Then after he did he invited me to Kingwood Church. I said to him, "Well, it's about time someone invited me to church."

I started attending Kingwood, and to say the least, they had to wear kid gloves around me because I was so wounded from churches that I attended not reaching out to me. I had gone off on a couple of people even when I first started attending Kingwood in 1999. However, I started to notice the more I went to that specific church I didn't hurt as much anymore. I came to God at Kingwood Church because of the unbearable pain. His healing love through the pastor and the members starting pushing out the rejection I felt.

MY AWESOME ITALIAN MAN

Ever since I was an adolescent, I had always wanted to marry an Italian man. I have always had a special place in my heart for Italy and the Italian culture. One day, a friend of mine told me to write down everything that I wanted in a husband. After having been through two horrific marital experiences and feeling like a defective woman I had to totally shift my mind into the fact that I could be happily married. Therefore, I put all the qualities in a desired mate down on paper.

During this time (August 2001) I was winding up my job with the outpatient psychiatry program as a therapist, and was getting ready to begin my studies in law school. A couple of weeks before I left, all of a sudden I started getting restlessness in my spirit to get on an Internet dating Web site. I thought to myself that God would not want me to get on an Internet dating Web site—that is *so* the devil. The restlessness continued; I felt like I could not breathe without the restlessness growing. Finally, I pointed my finger to the ceiling in my office and spoke out loud, "God I'm going to get on this Web site for dating so you will leave me alone and I will show you that this is of the devil."

However, immediately when I did register with the dating Web site, I had peace in my spirit and no more restlessness. As God had destined, I noticed this awesome man, Rich Gatto, on the Web site, and he was Italian! I so enjoyed the fact that there was a nice-looking Christian Italian man on the dating Web site. I never thought it would go into a serious relationship because he lived in Connecticut and I lived in Alabama. We started sending e-mails to each other and discovered that we had the same goals and values in life. Before I knew it, we started talking over the phone. Then one day, Rich said he wanted to meet me.

The funny thing, though, is that in my spirit I knew that this was my husband. This was the man that I had written all of the qualities about on that piece of paper and then some. This was my prince charming. Rich and I scheduled to meet in mid-August 2001. Right before we actually met, our conversation starting getting more serious, and we both knew that God had meant for us to wed. Before Rich ever came down to meet me for the first time, we planned our wedding for December 22, 2001. That's right. We were married four months after meeting face to face. There is no way to possibly describe our connection. All I can tell you is that I felt as though I had met Rich in Heaven, knowing that we would be married one day. I still had some residue of the alcohol in my life when Rich and I initially met in 2001 and it carried over into 2002. However, between wrestling for my deliverance from alcoholism and the love God poured out on me through Rich, I was set free.

I went on to receive my law degree, juris doctorate, and now use that degree in combination with my master's of social work in helping hurting families. My long-term desire is to be a state commissioner in a social welfare program and get involved in public office. I am a visionary; I have developed programs for those who have need and aspire to be in a position where I can use that gifting to help people in a public office. In addition, I am an ordained minister with my husband, Rich, in our ministry "22 IS 22" (Isaiah 22:22 Company) that we started in 2007 and in Princess Warriors, which is a women's ministry I started in 2005. I took time off between my second year and third year of law school in 2004 to write the "Glory to Glory Sisterhood" series.

The Glory to Glory Sisterhood

It was obvious by looking at my early years in high school that I had never cared if I was accepted by others. However, all through the first 15 years of my adult life—from college leading up to my total commitment to God—I was lost in a mix of emotions. I desired to be like the fearless young lady that I remembered from high school, but I also desired acceptance. My need for both was strong.

What I have come to discover is that God the Father has placed in each of us a desire to be accepted, because in Him that is what we are—fully accepted. He is our Beloved, and He accepts us no matter what we have done. In addition, I have found that I wanted to be separate from others because our Father has called his children a royal priesthood, a peculiar people. This was a paradox, because I wanted to be accepted but separate.

In pursuing God, I have discovered through the teachings of Jesus that many times His ways are paradoxical to our ways. To keep your life, you have to lose it. To be the greatest, you have to be the least. To get, you first have to give, and so many more. The Holy Spirit then showed me a sisterhood where a woman can be both accepted and separate—the sisterhood established in Christ.

New Journey

I am asking every girl and woman to take this journey with me, rediscovering your rightful place on earth as a daughter of the Most High God and a joint heir with Christ.

> *Now if we are children, then we are heirs—heirs of God and co-heirs with Christ, if indeed we share in His sufferings in order that we may also share in His glory* (Romans 8:17 NIV).

It is my hope that all of you can go through a healing process in which old wounds will be cleansed and filled with the Great Physician's medicine of love and acceptance. God is so good about loving the hurt out of us. Every woman is an honorable vessel unto the Lord, and it is with great love that I desire to be an instrument to bring women together. We have grown up competing with each other in cheerleading, dance teams, boyfriends, and so on. I believe we must come to a new understanding of how sisters are to act and what they are to do. The only way to demonstrate this is to start from what sisters do and don't do and then walk through who we are in Christ. In later books, we will also uncover devices the enemy uses in order to bring us down. When we are finished, I hope that we can all find certainty of who we are in Christ and become sensitive to the move of the Holy Spirit while being alerted to the schemes of the enemy.

Creating Your Story

QUESTIONS:

1. Recall godly behaviors that you liked about yourself while growing up. Were you kind, joyful, giving, longsuffering, forbearing, patient, etc.? How old were you when you exhibited these behaviors?

2. Identify lies that the enemy told you about yourself while you were growing up. For example, you may have heard lies telling you that you were ugly, unlovable, worthless, a bad girl, clumsy, etc.

3. Did the lies from the enemy change the godly behaviors that you had? If the answer is yes, go to the next question. If not, identify how God protected you from the enemy's lies.

4. What were the behaviors that accompanied each lie? For example, if the enemy told you that you were ugly, did you start speaking that you were ugly, accepting comments that called you ugly, and avoiding the mirror? What ungodly behaviors resulted (drinking, being promiscuous, unwholesome talk, eating disorders, etc.)?

5. What ungodly behaviors do you presently have that you need God to change? What godly behaviors did you have as a youth that you want God to restore?

6. Write your story:

What
Sisters Do

SECTION TWO

As a result of this revelation that God wants to make us feel accepted and separate, I have been led by His Holy Spirit to share His heart. I want to show you that there is a sisterhood that allows us to strive for the same things, all while encouraging each other to reach the prize of the "high call." I have chosen to call this sisterhood, "The Glory to Glory Sisterhood," which is taken from the Scripture in Second Corinthians:

> *Now the Lord is that Spirit: and where the Spirit of the Lord is, there is liberty. But we all, with open face beholding as in*

a glass the glory of the Lord, are changed into the same image from glory to glory, even as by the Spirit of the Lord (2 Corinthians 3:17-18 KJV).

GOD'S VOICE

For since the creation of the world God's invisible qualities— His eternal power and divine nature—have been clearly seen, being understood from what has been made, so that men are without excuse (Romans 1:20 NIV).

God makes His invisible Self visible to us in His creation. Things that might seem to have nothing to do with God actually have much to say about Him. For example, order is brought to our streets through signs so that we can be prepared to go a certain speed, prepare for a light, or watch for children at play or men working on the roads. God's Holy Spirit has shown me through these simple signs that there is so much He wants us to "see."

He has shown me that we are to watch the "children at play." God speaks to us in the simple games children play in the yard or fields. For instance, the game hide and seek can refer to Him or to the lost. God wants us to "seek" Him, and the Word says that when a man found a treasure in a field, he sold all he had to get it.

Again, the Kingdom of Heaven is like treasure hidden in a field, which a man found and hid; and for joy over it he goes and sells all that he has and buys that field (Matthew 13:44).

In addition, God wants His children to find those that are hidden from Him, not because He doesn't see them, but because by sin, they have hidden themselves from God and cut off the divine fellowship. For another example, in the game Red Rover the Holy Spirit showed me that we Kingdom brothers and sisters were standing together, hand in hand, calling out to the other side, the lost. We were telling them to come join the family, and we were supposed to hold tightly and not let them break our bond so that they, in turn, could join us.

God also makes Himself visible to us in fraternal organizations (sororities and fraternities). What lessons that speak of God can we learn from these organizations? First, they are "family" so to speak—a sisterhood. Next, they prefer each other to other women outside of their sorority. Finally, there is a mentorship program inside of the sorority that allows the older sisters to mentor the younger ones, known as "big sister" and "little sister" ties. Let's look deeper at these connections between fraternal organizations and the family of God.

Family

My Sister

When we look at other women, our first thought should be "My Sister." My actual sister, Liz Anne Elsea, is six years younger than me. I know that there were times that we had our petty childish arguments growing up, but she and I were close in the fact that we cared for each other as sisters. I love my sister, Liz Anne, as a real sister because that's what she is. Through the years we have connected in a manner that we encourage and edify each other not only as natural sisters but also spiritual sisters. This has made our relationship even deeper and richer. Likewise, God wants His daughters to see each other as sisters because you will do things for a sister that you might not do for other women. Liz Anne would keep my oldest son, Christopher, when I got in a tight spot and needed her too. She would also give me gifts that I might not be able to afford at the time, especially during law school when I could not work. She also prayed for me during the time I was divorced and an alcoholic when other women would not even think about it. A sister will do a lot more for you than other women who are not your sister. Therefore, as spiritual sisters God wants us to do the very same thing as if the other woman was our natural sister, our real sister. God wants us to treat each other like real sisters.

In a sorority, you will not find a variety of women from all sorts of other groups. Instead, a sorority is made up of women that have been chosen and have decided to join one group. Likewise, we sisters in Christ are similar. We have been chosen by God before the foundations of the earth.

> *Before I formed you in the womb I knew you; before you were born I sanctified you...* (Jeremiah 1:5).

We establish our familial tie when we make a decision to accept Christ. In our acceptance of Christ—the doorway to the Kingdom of God—we are made a part of the sisterhood. When we leave our old life for the new life of citizenship in the Kingdom of God, we take on the new order and are a part of the new family, thus making us daughters of God and joint heirs with Christ.

> *The Spirit Himself bears witness with our spirit that we are children of God, and if children, then heirs—heirs of God and joint heirs with Christ, if indeed we suffer with Him, that we may also be glorified together* (Romans 8:16-17).

This makes us family; it makes us sisters.

This is different from sororities, however, because there are only so many women that the sorority can accept into their group each year. Therefore, if they can only accept 30 new girls each August and 400 go through rush, that will mean that 370 will not make it into the sorority. The Glory to Glory Sisterhood is not limited by number. Instead, it is the desire of our heavenly Father that all might be saved:

> *...who desires all men to be saved and to come to the knowledge of the truth* (1 Timothy 2:4).

He wants us to carry the gospel to the ends of the world:

> *And Jesus came and spoke to them, saying, "All authority has been given to Me in Heaven and on earth. Go therefore and make disciples of all the nations, baptizing them in the name of the Father and of the Son and of the Holy Spirit, teaching them to observe all things that I have commanded you; and lo, I am with you always, even to the end of the age." Amen* (Matthew 28:18-20).

Thus we see that all women, young ladies, and girls are accepted into the family. When they decide to join the family, their membership is certain.

SORORITY RUSH

During my rush experience in my first year of college, there was one group that I particularly wanted to pursue. However, they cut me after the first day of rush. Other groups that I knew I did not want to join offered me invitations to continue possible membership with them. Unlike human-made sororities, God will not cut us from the Glory to Glory Sisterhood. It is His desire to offer us membership for our entire lives, and Christ continually knocks on our heart's door, urging us to establish our place in the sisterhood.

> *Behold, I stand at the door and knock. If anyone hears My voice and opens the door, I will come in to him and dine with him, and he with Me* (Revelation 3:20).

So you can see how the sisterhood in a sorority speaks of our sisterhood in Christ. The main difference between the sorority rush and the Glory to Glory Sisterhood is unlimited membership. Whereas human sororities have to carefully pick new sisters and can only choose a certain number, the sisterhood established in Christ merely requires that we make a decision for Him, accepting Him as our Lord and Savior. Then, we become part of a glorious sisterhood, because He has already chosen us before the foundations of the earth.

CHURCH IN THE SISTERHOOD

As a result of our newfound sisterhood in Christ Jesus it is necessary for us to get involved in a local church. There are many churches that a sister can choose from. The word of God states that we will flourish if we are planted in the house of the Lord (see Psalm 92:13). I have discovered that when I would stay planted in a church that I would grow more spiritually. I was not a person to jump around from church to church growing up. I attended one church for a couple of years as a young first and second grader in Columbus, Mississippi. After my mom and dad moved to Meridian I started attending a church there in my elementary years and continued there until I graduated from high school and went to college. When I moved to Jackson, Mississippi, I attended a church there a few years until I moved on the other side of the city and found a church closer by. Then when I moved to Birmingham I attended a church there for five years until I came to Kingwood Church where I have been since 1999. In each location that I was planted for years I was able to grow a lot in the Lord, especially at Kingwood. I did go down a wrong path during college and my years as a single mother but I did not stop attending church because I knew that it was my connection in God's house that would keep me in a place of growth and flourishing in time.

People who jump from church to church are like a plant that is planted in one place and then uprooted and planted in another place and then yet uprooted and planted in another place. A plant that continues in this state is unhealthy and does not grow as well as a plant that is placed in one location for years and grows there. That is why it is necessary to find a church home and stay planted there. God will show you the place that will be your church home if you ask Him to.

CHURCH FAMILY

I found out then when I started attending a church I felt as though they were my family, and in God's Kingdom the local church is our family. My favorite times growing up as a youth were spent at Southside Baptist Church in Meridian, Mississippi. My mom and dad were involved in many areas of the church and took my brother, David, my sister, Liz Anne, and myself every time the church doors were open.

I became very involved in the youth group there and in the youth choir. I was able to sing solos for special music during the evening services and I remember many times my father and mother helping me prepare and coaching me for those special solos. In the youth group we went to Six Flags in Atlanta, Georgia, youth missions trips, and state assemblies. Those young people had become my family, too. We treated each other like brothers and sisters.

Now, at Kingwood Church, I have been there since 1999 and now serve in a life group, God Quest, that I have been a part of for over five years when it came into existence. My husband, Rich, and I had been in another Sunday school group but knew that God wanted us to go into God Quest once it started. Since being in God Quest, I have grown leaps and bounds. I am now one of the teachers in the class. On occasion, I teach in other areas of the church or otherwise volunteer, and my sons Christopher and Matthew were able to grow up in that church, as I did when I went to Southside Baptist.

Kingwood Church has become as close to me as my own family. There are women there who I have laughed with, cried with, rejoiced with, worshiped with. The same is true for my husband and children. All I can say is that I have grown incredibly from being involved with a local church family and you sister will too.

God's Bold Sisterhood

This is a sisterhood where no one is left out by choice but all are accepted. It is a place where, even though a sister may fall and make bad decisions, the rest of the sisters will intercede on her behalf, asking for mercy and grace for the weaker sister.

We can see a picture of this in the military when soldiers are in combat mode. While fighting on the front lines, troops go into enemy territory expecting to make an impact with their war tactics. If one of their own gets hurt and has fallen, they do not leave that soldier behind. Many military men and women will testify that it is unacceptable to leave a fallen comrade behind in battle. A fallen comrade doesn't speak of a troop that is strong and doing well, but one that has gotten attacked while in battle.

God does not want anything less from us as His daughters. If He sees one of His fallen daughters in bondage to the enemy, He wants His stronger daughters to be there for her. He is training up warriors, not wimps. God is an almighty force, and He expects us to take our sister out of bondage by force (see Matt. 11:12).

In Old Testament times, people were afraid of the Jews. I can only imagine that others would tremble and back up, standing and pointing in awe saying, "They are God's people," fearing to offend the Jews and have the wrath of God come upon them.

PRINCESS WARRIORS

In the same manner, we as daughters of God ought to have this mind-set. As women in Christ we are a chosen people, separated from the rest of the world. We stand and walk together in unity and not in division. We need to understand who we are in Christ, even if we do not see ourselves as warriors. Although we are female, we are made warriors in Him. Therefore, when we see a sister in Christ in bondage to sin (alcoholism, drugs, anger, and so on), we should not leave her behind; we should put the *tallit* over her—covering her with the grace of God—and stand beside her.

> *Brethren, if anyone among you wanders from the truth, and someone turns him back, let him know that he who turns a sinner from the error of his way will save a soul from death and cover a multitude of sins* (James 5:19-20).

Being in the Family

QUESTIONS:

1. Do you go to church regularly? If not, can you do something in order to find a church home and attend regularly?

2. Do you have a problem jumping from one church to another? If so, what can you do in order to prevent that from happening? For example, offense is a reason why most of us become discontent and leave churches. Can you make a commitment that you will not leave a church, no matter what you are offended by or discontented with? Can you commit to staying at a church in the midst of the discomfort? If you do, you will grow incredibly.

3. What do you have to offer the church? Are you creative, good with administrative duties, a good helper, etc.?

4. Is there an area in which you can contribute in any small way to your local church? Can you make phone calls, help the women's ministry, pray for others, be a greeter, etc.? Do not commit to anything without counting the cost. Make sure that you do not neglect any obligations that you already have with your own family (your husband, children, etc.).

5. Do you have sisters whom you meet with regularly? Going to church alone is not enough; you need to have women you can depend on to talk to and pray with.

c h a p t e r

4

Preference of Sisters over Non-Sisters

HAVING A CONNECTION

Let us hold fast the confession of our hope without wavering, for He who promised is faithful. And let us consider one another in order to stir up love and good works, not forsaking the assembling of ourselves together, as is the manner of some, but exhorting one another, and so much the more as you see the Day approaching (Hebrews 10:23-25).

On any university campus, you can see sorority sisters preferring each other to non–sorority sisters. This behavior results from the close ties made among sorority sisters in college. If a lady from a sorority enters a new class and sees a sister from her sorority, she doesn't have to know her well or have a deep bond with her to be drawn to sit by her, because there is an understanding between the two ladies of what they belong to—the sorority. Their sorority has a certain secret that is only revealed to the women in that sorority at initiation. In addition, the sorority members work toward a common goal, promoting their sorority favorably among others and speaking well of their sorority sisters. Although there might not be a close bond between the sorority sisters, membership alone is the connection that brings a knowing and a comfort. Thus, it is reasonable that they prefer their own sorority sisters to others.

STRENGTH AND ENCOURAGEMENT

In the same manner, we sisters in Christ ought to prefer each other to those not in the sisterhood. In order to understand this, we must be tuned in to the Holy Spirit. For example, when women in the workplace are making lunch buddies or office buddies, it is a natural tendency for sisters in Christ to gravitate toward each other. This is not to say that we do not associate with nonbelievers. There is a Holy Spirit "assignment time" which requires us to work with those not in Christ.

The Word says to build each other up in edification and fellowship (see Heb. 10:25). "Fellowship" is defined as "companionship; a mutual sharing, as of experience, interests; company."[1] The mutual sharing and experience that brings us together as sisters is that we are of the same family—the Family of Christ. This gives us a common experience, interest, and company with each other. That is why many Christian women who work in the same office eat together and share breaks together—because underneath the suits and office positions, there is an unspoken knowing that they are really sisters in Christ, and this brings a connection. They meet and desire each other's company because of their membership in the sisterhood. For the most part, these women will be edifying each other, speaking words of encouragement, discussing the Word of the Lord, and giving testimony of what God is doing in their life.

No Hypocrite

Many people look at Christian women and want to place a label on them, saying that "Christian women" are not being "Christian" if they are not spending time with everyone. Some people might frown on Christian women fellowshiping with each other in the secular world and actually think that they are "less Christian." We do not need to let the enemy fool us. If there is an area where we feel the pressure of the world, then most likely it is not of God. Remember that God's ways are above our ways, and Jesus brought correction to the Pharisees and their futile traditional ways.

> *For as the heavens are higher than the earth, **so are My ways higher than your ways, and My thoughts than your thoughts*** (Isaiah 55:9).

The Word tells us to prefer each other to nonbelievers; the world tells us that if we are not associating with everyone then we are hypocrites. We must be sensitive to the Holy Spirit in order to determine if we are to fellowship with each other or be on assignment to witness to non-believers. At times, we should fellowship with each other, pulling out the gifts of God to strengthen each other, and other times we are on assignment from the Lord, either individually or in groups, working to reach out to a lost and dying world. For example, when I have lunch dates or coffee times with my sisters in Christ I know that it is a time for us to edify each other in the Lord. I know it is not a time for me to worry about if a nonbeliever is there. My friend, Jenny, is a sister that I enjoy coffee times with. During those times, we exhort each other in the Lord and listen to what the Lord has been saying to each of us. In the midst of our meeting there are times that the gift of exhortation is pulled out in each of us and we leave our meeting feeling as if we have had a full spiritual buffet with the Holy Spirit.

On other occasions, there have been times when I have gone to a restaurant with one of my sisters in the Lord and sense the Holy Spirit drawing either a waitress or another customer to us. In that occasion, my sisters and I have witnessed and ministered to many women who were not serving the Lord but had started getting hungry and thirsty for the righteousness of Christ Jesus. In those occasions, we were on an assignment for the Lord to bring the Gospel, the Good News.

SECRET AGENT

When we do Kingdom work, we might feel a knowing in our spirit that we have an individual assignment with a nonbeliever. Other times, a couple of sisters in Christ might have an assignment to carry out together.

> *Sanctify them through Thy truth: Thy Word is truth. As Thou hast sent Me into the world, even so have **I also sent them into the world.** And for their sakes I sanctify Myself, that they also might be sanctified through the truth* (John 17:17-19 KJV).

For an analogy that describes individual versus team effort, compare war movies to secret agent movies. In a war movie, we usually see a team effort carrying out a strategic war tactic that requires the troop to work together in attacking the enemy. However, in a secret agent movie, one special agent is sent to weaken the enemy or carry out the assignment.

AN ASSIGNMENT

Jesus sent us out into the world to do incredible things for the work of the Kingdom (see Matt. 28:19-20). It is His desire that we go forward and do greater things than He did.

> *Verily, verily, I say unto you, he that believeth on Me, the works that I do shall he do also; and greater works than these shall he do; because I go unto My Father* (John 14:12 KJV).

An assignment God had me on, as one who was like a secret agent with was a woman in her mid-forties, Allison. When most people looked at Allison they would see a crazy woman who acted like she was 17 and made sure that everyone knew it. Most people abhorred being anywhere in the vicinity that Allison was because she was very loud and demonstrative in everything. Moreover, most of the time she had been drinking vodka. This woman had a son who attended the school my oldest son went to.

During that time, the Holy Spirit started showing me that Allison was in bondage due to a lot of pain that she had been through in her life where the enemy had brought rejection against her. As a result, she was a social outcast. Without much warning, God would line it up so that I would happen to be in a place where Allison was. In those occasions I start having a conversation with her regarding things that were going on in her life. In one of those instances, we were at our sons' Christmas concert and she had been drinking and was very loud. I asked her if she would sit by me and my husband. I knew that many were shocked that I wanted this lady to sit by me. The Holy Spirit told me that it was necessary in order for her to understand the love and acceptance of Christ Jesus. If she would see a woman like me, who was dressed nice and went to church who wanted to hang around her, then she would know that Jesus was no different. Jesus wanted to hang around Allison, too.

It was during that time that Allison poured out her whole life story, and my heart melted at what had happened to this woman, who was made in the image of God. I knew that God wanted Allison to walk into His Everlasting Love, to receive the healing that I did.

On other occasions, I would see Allison, with no visible change yet, continuing to be loud, and still treated as an outcast by others. God would continue to line it up for us to make contact. Once I was at a gas station and I saw Allison coming out. Getting out of my car, I went up to her and told her how beautiful she was to God. That God loved her and thought the world of her and wanted her to know that in Jesus Christ she was accepted. Allison stood there holding her case of beer and wept. The meetings that Jenny and I had were only for the building up of each other in Jesus. However, when I would share the Gospel and God's love to Allison, I felt just as built up as I did with Jenny. It was because as a Secret Agent for God in sharing His love to Allison, I literally could feel His loving being poured into me onto her, and she received it because she was so desperate and hungry for love. The enemy, the devil, had no clue that before the foundations of the earth, God would line things up so that I could be His secret weapon to reach Allison. Today, I'm not sure if Allison is still living here, but I know that God has another one of His daughters picking up where I left off with her.

ANGEL OF LIGHT

This area of preferring one another is one where deception can easily creep in. Remember that satan is not going to come with a pitch fork and fire brewing under him; rather, he is going to come as an angel of light. He might use a non-believer to divide sisters in Christ. One of the strongest weapons against the enemy is agreement between two sisters in Christ.

> *Again I say unto you, that if two of you shall agree on earth as touching any thing that they shall ask, it shall be done for them of My Father which is in Heaven. For where two or three are gathered together in My name, there am I in the midst of them* (Matthew 18:19-20 KJV).

We need to guard our relationships with our sisters. If we see division caused by an unbeliever rising between sisters, then we are to bring it under Holy Spirit counsel immediately and ask for wisdom. Most likely, if we only meet with our sister in Christ for a time, we will find the relationship strengthened and the focus of our Kingdom purpose back on course. For example, in one of my former positions as a social worker there was a woman with whom I did a Bible study in the mornings. She and I met some mornings and felt the Holy Spirit move in the midst of our time together. Eventually, this nonbeliever who was very much in the world started detesting the fact that I was not spending time with her. I thought I could influence her with my Christian walk, but what I found was that she had no hunger or thirst for righteousness. Rather, she only mocked Christians and their living for the Lord. Her desire to spend time with me was not for me to influence her, but rather, for her to influence me. Before I knew it, I was tolerating some of the ungodly language and discussion she would often speak about. Eventually, I started feeling dirty and did not know why. Then my eyes were opened to the fact that the enemy had sent this lady in to bring division between me and another woman, dividing up our time studying the Bible together. This is what satan does. He wants to trick you sometimes into influencing a nonbeliever for Christ but the Holy Spirit has not quickened the woman to thirst and hunger for the righteousness of Christ Jesus. Rather, the woman instead is so deep in the world and has nothing but a desire for things of the world and is not ready for the things of Christ. If we are not careful, they can influence us instead of us influencing them.

GUILTY

The enemy is intent on making us feel like "bad girls," and he is going to do it by laying a worldly guilt trip on us. We see this when we start feeling bad because others criticize us for meeting with our sister in Christ or call us a snob for not tolerating their off-color jokes and worldly behaviors.

> *How that they told you there should be mockers in the last time, who should walk after their own ungodly lusts. These be they who separate themselves, sensual, having not the Spirit* (Jude 1:18-19 KJV).

Recognize that, again, anytime you are feeling pressure, it is usually of the world and not of God. It is a time to be still and get counsel from the Holy Spirit to see what the truth is in regards to the situation. Most likely, the enemy is trying to make us feel bad and is pressuring us to perform in our flesh. When we operate in the flesh, we are going against the will of the Father. Maintain a position of hearing God.

How to Be a Better Sister

QUESTIONS

1. Do you have problems interacting with other women?

2. What can you ask God to change in you to make you a better sister? For example, can you be more patient, a better listener, more selfless, etc.?

3. Are you pressured by the world when it comes to preferring your sister in Christ? For example, when you are at work or at a women's group, do you feel guilty when you want to spend time with your sister? If you do feel guilty, what situation creates that feeling?

4. What do you need to do to withstand the pressures of the world and be more committed to your sisters?

5. Do you and your sisters ever share Jesus with other women? If not, why? How can you overcome your reasons?

6. Are you praying for nonbelievers?

ENDNOTE

1. *Webster's New World Dictionary of the American Language* 2nd College Edition (New York: Prentice Hall Press, 1986).

c h a p t e r

5

Mentorship in the Sisterhood

Big Sister, Little Sister

In sororities there is a "big sister, little sister" relationship whereby a new woman adopted into the sorority is given an "older sister" to be her mentor.

> *Likewise, teach the older women to be reverent in the way they live, not to be slanderers or addicted to much wine, but to teach what is good. Then they can train the younger women to love their husbands and children, to be self-controlled and pure, to be busy at home, to be kind, and to be subject to their husbands, so that no one will malign the word of God* (Titus 2:3-5 NIV).

In the Glory to Glory Sisterhood, the older women of the church are to train up and mentor the younger women. Younger women are to learn how to be good wives, mothers, daughters, friends, and women in Christ. All women are to be the ideal woman, because God the Father designed us to be wonderful; we are "fearfully and wonderfully made."

> *I will praise You, for I am fearfully and wonderfully made;*
> *marvelous are Your works, and that my soul knows very well*
> (Psalms 139:14).

It is His desire to show us who we are in Him and what we are able to do. This is pictured beautifully in the mentoring relationship between older and younger women in Christ.

I have heard it said that the reason so many older husbands are running around with younger women is because the older wives have not mentored the young women; they have left the world to. The world teaches them to look sexy, stay up late, live for self, make a lot of money, marry a rich man even if he is already married, and have babies but act as though they are a burden, among other things. The world is training up the younger women, and as a result, they are a product of the world. One of my favorite teachers in this regard is Lisa Bevere, author of, among other things, a book about sexual purity before marriage, *"Kissed the Girls and Made Them Cry."*

Stop Eating and Start Serving

We as older, more mature women in Christ (I was born in the mid-sixties) have to make ourselves available for the younger women in Christ. Instead of being so caught up in attending meetings to get a word, a teaching, or some encouragement, we need to be the ones to sow a word, to teach, or to encourage younger women. If we take the time to do what was demonstrated in the Old and New Testament, then we will see unity in the sisterhood. Then, if a sister strays off the beaten path, even if a mentor is not there to guide her, a younger lady who has been properly mentored can step out to guide her because of the instruction she received.

I have mentored several women ranging from 18 to 63 years old. While mentoring, I have had opportunity to speak into women's lives whenever they might have backslidden from the Lord, and because of our relationship they did not feel judged but rather loved. Each relationship where I am mentoring another woman is individualized to that person. For example, there are a couple of women I am mentoring to do ministry. I have met with women individually to mentor them in ministering anything from deliverance to bringing out their gifts. Moreover, my ministry "Princess Warriors" equips women to minister to others.

In addition, there are some women I mentor as a "life coach." They might share financial struggles, marital issues, raising children, other relational issues, seeking a job or education. These women have truly been grateful for my time and efforts. I do not charge anything for this, but rather give it freely as I have been mentored, too.

This past Christmas season (2009), I was sitting with my family watching a movie. My doorbell rang and one of the ladies I mentored stood in the dark with a small gold box in her hand. This particular lady is so hungry and thirsty for righteousness. She handed it to me and said, "I had to make sure you got this," hugged my neck and left. She did not have much to offer financially. When I opened the box, there was an antique perfume necklace. On the note, she said that when she saw this she had to get it for me and knew that I could put my anointing oil in it for ministering. I cannot begin to express the joy and the love that flooded me when I opened the box and read the note. That one gift is my favorite Christmas present ever. I felt as though that woman had given her very all to me for the work of the Lord in mentoring her.

It is through this important relationship that knowledge and truth are passed. Christ told us to go and make disciples, and the way to make a disciple is through training them, which requires time and all the fruits of the spirit.

> But the fruit of the Spirit is love, joy, peace, longsuffering, gentleness, goodness, faith, meekness, temperance: against such there is no law (Galatians 5:22-23 KJV).

The Two Widows

My favorite story that depicts the mentoring relationship is that of Ruth and Naomi in the book of Ruth. Ruth had already returned to Bethlehem with Naomi. Naomi returned a depressed woman, having lost her husband and her two sons. Ruth, her widowed daughter-in-law, followed Naomi because of the God she served. Actually, Ruth clung to Naomi, and Naomi initially prompted her to not follow her to Bethlehem (see Ruth 1:14). Ruth replied to Naomi:

> *"Entreat me not to leave you, or to turn back from following after you; for wherever you go, I will go; and wherever you lodge, I will lodge; your people shall be my people, and your God, my God. Where you die, I will die, and there will I be buried. The Lord do so to me, and more also, if anything but death parts you and me." When she saw that she was determined to go with her, she stopped speaking to her* (Ruth 1:16-18).

It was *after* Naomi saw Ruth's determination that Naomi stopped urging her. Sometimes it takes determination from a younger woman to give the older woman a reason to mentor her.

I was asked to mentor some younger women. Initially I agreed, excited at the prospect of being a mentor since it was new for me. However, I later discovered that some women did not keep their appointments. At the time, I was working in a home business with my husband, being a wife to my husband and a mother to my children, being involved in an international ministry, and pursuing a law degree. To say the least, my time was very valuable, and to carve out any time was a sacrifice. I would go through great effort to arrange my schedule, yet there would be occasions when someone would back out and not give me a call until that day, if they called at all.

Ruth was an example of a mentor's ideal "trainee." She was determined and her eyes were set like flint to receive instruction from Naomi. As a mentee, you should make sure to keep all scheduled appointments and give timely notice to your mentor if it is possible, so that she can fully use her valuable time. What is more, there might be another young woman who is desperate for mentoring and is unable to receive an appointment.

A word to those who are mentoring other women: It is out of experience that I only work with the "Ruth's" of the church (church referring to believers). This doesn't dismiss the times that I provide one-on-one over the telephone, in person after a meeting or church service, or in the grocery store if necessary for those I'm not mentoring. However, the ones that I carve time out for are those who are determined to receive teaching and are hungry and willing to be accountable to me, the mentor.

BE THE WOMAN YOU ALWAYS WANTED TO BE

For those women who have not been mentored, do not fret. Remember that His grace is sufficient. As I've heard stated by Lisa Bevere, we need to become the woman that we've always *wanted* to have come and mentor us. Seek first the Kingdom of God, and everything will be added unto you (see Matt. 6:32-34). As for me, I pursued God with all that was within me because I didn't have a mentor until 2004. I became the woman that I wanted to become before I received a mentor. Therefore, I obtained much of the instruction set out in Titus 2:3-5 by studying the Bible and reading books that were a complement to what I desired to learn. This Scripture paints a picture of the well-trained woman, stating she will know how to love her husband and children, be self-controlled and pure, keep busy at home, be kind, and be subject to her husband.

SEEKING GOD

In 2002, I became desperate for more of God. My hunger level increased until I was attending every Bible study possible and devouring Christian books placed in front of me. Every book John Bevere had written helped to feed my insatiable appetite for the Lord. I read his wife's books, as well as many by Joyce Meyer, Tony Evans, Neil T. Anderson, George Bloomer, Beth Moore, Tommy Tenny, Mark Rutland, David Wilkerson, Bruce Wilkinson, Paula White, T.D. Jakes, and others. I consumed their knowledge of God and sought out a group of women under whom I could sit. This group of women consisted of the wiser, elderly women, and I was nearly 30 years younger than they were. I took each crumb that came out of their mouths and sought God with diligence.

My search to become the woman I wanted to be started by finding out who I was in Christ and what my relationship was with the Holy God. My foundation was established much like building a home, and the very strength and bottom part of my foundation was the "fear of the Lord."

The fear of the Lord is the beginning of wisdom, and the knowledge of the Holy One is understanding (Proverbs 9:10).

I pursued the Holy God by looking through the lens of reverential fear.

I accelerated my maturity in Christ by first gaining a foundation on who God was; second, learning that my redemption was through Jesus Christ; and third, understanding that I had the empowerment to live as the Titus woman through His Holy Spirit. I have to admit that before I truly had the fear of the Lord, it was not as easy for me to really hear and see what God wanted me to know.

It is the very Spirit of God—the Spirit of the fear of the Lord—where wisdom and understanding come in to help the believer (see Isa. 11:2). I began to see that if I was not doing the will of the Father set out in the Word of God, then I was not pleasing Him and was in rebellion, which is witchcraft (see 1 Sam. 15:23). Therefore, I sought out what God wanted me to be—a princess daughter.

GOD TAUGHT ME

I discovered that He liked my being submitted to my husband, although to the world it might seem as though I was "weak." God taught me that I was not being obedient when I sought things through self-seeking ambition instead of godly ambition. He taught me that my children were a huge blessing from Him, and that I was not only to be appreciative, kind, and loving to them, but I was also to respect them as honorable vessels unto the Lord. He taught me that through the furnace of affliction (losing everything financially and my son nearly dying) and tribulation all things which were vile and impure could be burned out of me, and I would end up becoming more like Jesus. He taught me that I was to possess the fruits of the Spirit at all times, and if I was operating outside of them then I was in disobedience to His Word (see Gal. 5:22-25).

Not having a mentor need not stop you from becoming the best you can be in Christ. A great thing that has come from my pursuing God is that both older and younger women now come to me and ask me mentoring advice in regard to their relationships with their husbands, children, businesses, and so on. It is so incredible that I was actually burning in my desire for God only a year and a half before this began. However, because of my submission to God and His will for my life, He put me on the pathway of acceleration.

> *And a highway will be there; it will be called the Way of Holiness. The unclean will not journey on it; it will be for those who walk in that Way; wicked fools will not go about on it. No lion will be there, nor will any ferocious beast get up on it; they will not be found there. But only the redeemed will walk there* (Isaiah 35:8-9 NIV).

God is no respecter of persons and will do the same for any woman who pursues Him.

MAMA SHEILA

The first type of mentoring I received was not geared toward becoming a good Titus woman—loving wife, good mother, pure, and so on. Instead, I was being mentored in how to minister to others and how to be sensitive to the move of the Holy Spirit. My first mentor, Sheila Guidry (whom I called "Mama Sheila"), pushed me to do ministry when I would otherwise hold back or not move in my gifting. She supported my stepping out in faith to minister, and she was there for me with prayer, a fresh word and guidance in operating under the unction of the Holy Spirit, as well as to hold me accountable. I'm grateful for her mentorship in the area of ministry, but it would never have been possible so soon if I had not pursued God and a lifestyle of holiness with everything in me.

Sheila is well known by others and I consider it an honor to have been under her training. Let me make it clear that I am far from where I would like to be. I continually go through the process of submitting to the surgery table to allow another character ungodly trait to be pulled out of my heart.

However, I'm so pleased that I'm closer to being where I would like than I was three years ago, two years ago, and even one month ago.

To sum up, sororities depict three areas in which God desires for His daughters to grow. They are being a family (sisters), preferring each other to nonbelievers, and the mentoring relationship. In order to be a part of the Glory to Glory Sisterhood, we have to give ourselves to being a part of a family, preferring our sister, and being in a mentoring relationship.

Big Sister, Little Sister

QUESTIONS:

1. Do you have a mentor? If not, can you seek out a godly, mature woman whom can mentor you?

2. Are you teachable? When a mentor corrects you, do you get offended or angry? If you do get angry then you need to work on being more teachable.

3. Are you accountable?

4. Are you able to be a mentor? If not, is it because you need to grow more in the Lord? If you are ready, can you pray for God to send you the women He wants you to mentor? Make sure that if you choose to mentor others, you operate under your own mentor or strong Christian sister, and be accountable to her about your mentoring.

What Sisters
Don't Do

SECTION THREE

We have been discussing what sisters in Christ do, but we must also delineate what we don't do. Until we receive both sides of the truth, we only walk in half-truths. God firmly establishes by His Word not only "thou shall" but also "thou shall not." This means that there are acts that we are to do and others that we are to refrain from doing. It is not my intention to bring condemnation to anyone, because condemnation is of the enemy, satan. God does not condemn but instead convicts through His Holy Spirit. If you feel "sharpness" in your spirit while reading this chapter, understand that it is God's Holy Spirit tugging on your heart in order to get a specific area of sin out of your life and to close the door on it.

At the end of the section, I will lead us in prayer to repent from any sin, whether occasional or frequent. To "repent" literally means to change one's mind and turn away.[1] We have to change our mind about our sin and the way we view it, and if we see it as vile and sinful unto the Lord, then we will reject it. I commend all women for seeking the truth and going forward to receive cleansing and a change of mind and heart.

ENDNOTE

1. *Webster's New World Dictionary on the English Language,* 2nd College Edition (New York: Prentice Hall Press, 1986).

6

Gossip

*Furthermore, since they did not think it worthwhile to retain the knowledge of God, He gave them over to a depraved mind, to do what ought not to be done. They have become filled with every kind of wickedness, evil, greed and depravity. They are full of envy, murder, strife, deceit and malice. They **are gossips, slanderers**, God-haters, insolent, arrogant and boastful; they invent ways of doing evil; they disobey their parents; they are senseless, faithless, heartless, ruthless. Although they know God's righteous decree that those who do such things deserve death, they not only continue to do these very things but also approve of those who practice them (Romans 1:28-32 NIV).*

WORTHY OF DEATH

The Word puts gossips, whisperers, and backbiters in the same category with the unrighteous, fornicators, wicked people, murders, inventors of evil, covenant breakers, and so on. The Word says that they are unmerciful and without understanding. Their actions are worthy of death. It states that they not only take pleasure in gossiping but also approve of others who gossip.

As sisters in Christ, we never need to gossip about another sister or anyone for that matter. It is easy to overlook in the church, because in doing Christian activities we can be lured into gossiping without realizing it. Our heart motives demonstrate if we are gossiping or are instead helping a sister in Christ.

"Let's Pray for Her"

Sometimes prayer can be motivated out of gossip instead of actual concern. For example, if there is a woman's Bible study group that meets together, gossip can erupt out of a prayer need. In this group, say one of the women happens to be out one day. The others might, out of a wrong motive, bring up a discussion about the missing sister and eventually get on a "let's pray for her" session. However, before getting to that point the group has inadvertently cursed her by talking about her "problems" with everyone else but her. This is hurtful and wrong, even though they seem to be doing the "Christian thing" by praying for her and feeling "concerned" about her.

What are our heart motives, and what did Christ say? If our heart motives are anything outside of lifting her up, we are out of the will of God. His desires for us operate from the position of love. In truth, when we discuss another sister's problems in detail, it is not out of love. We are sharing information to harm her reputation or discredit her walk. Genesis provides a good example in the case of Noah.

Cover Your Naked Sister

In Genesis 9:20-25, after Noah's family had left the ark following God's cleansing of the earth, Noah became drunk and was in a position in which he exposed himself (he was naked). One of his sons, Ham, saw this and went to tell the other two sons, causing embarrassment to Noah. However, the other two sons, Shem and Japheth, did not dare to look on Noah's nakedness and instead went into the room with a garment to cover their father.

In the same way, we are to cover up *any* of our sister's nakedness and not discuss it with the intention of "helping" her. We cover her with our prayer, our confidence, our standing on the Word, and our encouragement of her. In addition, we do not make ourselves part of gossip by listening. When we hear a sister being exposed, we are to immediately cover it up by telling others that we are to pray for her and not talk about her. If we do this, we not only cover our sister's sin, but we are also being a vessel of honor for the Lord by helping others to see what is required of us as sisters in Christ.

My pastor has also dealt with church gossip disguised as concern for another brother or sister in Christ who is in error. His response to the "concerned" person is to first stop them and then ask whether he can take this concern up with the person in error. Because of this practice, he has been able to eliminate spiritual gossip.

WITCHES AND KETTLES

If we have been initiating or participating in any gossip, we are to immediately repent and put it under the blood; we are practicing witchcraft because it is not the will of God to tear down. His will is to build up members of the Body.

> *He who speaks on his own does so to gain honor for himself, but he who works for the honor of the one who sent him is a man of truth; there is nothing false about him* (John 7:18 NIV).

If every time that we gossiped we imagined ourselves standing over a big black kettle putting in ingredients that would bring a curse upon our sister and moreover we were finding other witches to agree to the curse, it would offend us. However, until we look at this sin as heinous, we will continue to practice it; and after receiving this knowledge, we do so willfully.

> *If we deliberately keep on sinning after we have received the knowledge of the truth, no sacrifice for sins is left* (Hebrews 10:26 NIV).

Gossip About Your Sisters

QUESTIONS:

1. Do you gossip about other women?

2. Do you associate with other women who gossip?

3. Do you watch any television shows or read magazines that capitalize off of gossip? If so, which ones?

4. Do you edify other women? If so, how do you edify (words of encouragement, notes, etc.)? If not, then what can you do to edify other women?

5. What Scriptures can you use to edify others?

chapter

7

Pride

Pride is a strong spirit, especially among women, which is why we see covetous jealousy and competitiveness so strong among the female gender. It is pride that caused man to fall, and the enemy is aware that pride will continue to cause many of us to fall again. We need to confront this spirit and sin in our lives and allow the Great Physician to remove it from us.

THE APPLE

In the book of Genesis, pride crept into the Garden of Eden when satan presented to Eve the apple from the Tree of the Knowledge of Good and Evil. God told Adam that he was not to eat from the tree, which Adam communicated to Eve. However, satan tempted Eve to eat the fruit from the tree, telling her that she would be "like God"—knowing good and evil (see Gen. 3:4 NIV). This is a demonstration of pride. Webster's Dictionary defines pride as "an over high opinion of oneself; exaggerated self-esteem; conceit."

Many times we can be at risk of having an overly high opinion of ourselves when we start operating in the gifts of the Spirit. For example, I have the gift of exhortation, and when I operate in that gift it does draw others to me; they are lifted up and encouraged. Because I receive exhortation by the Spirit, I have to guard my thoughts lest I think it was "me." It simply was the Spirit of God operating through me as a vessel, giving a word of exhortation to another person in order to encourage her. I have caught myself on occasion reflecting on the encouragement I've given others, thinking about it more than I needed to. In the same manner, we need to make sure that, when we are operating in the gifts of the Spirit and our other God-given gifts, we do not think it is "us." We need to continually give all the glory to God. This is why Paul says that we are to forget those things that are behind and press forward to the high call.

> *Not that I have already obtained all this, or have already been made perfect, but I press on to take hold of that for which Christ Jesus took hold of me. Brothers, I do not consider myself yet to have taken hold of it. But one thing I do: Forgetting what is behind and straining toward what is ahead, I press on toward the goal to win the prize for which God has called me heavenward in Christ Jesus* (Philippians 3:12-14 NIV).

Most people think that he is referring to the mistakes we have made. However, he is talking about *all* things that are behind us, both good and bad. Are there any women who live in "those days"? It could be high school accomplishments, athletic achievements, college days, or many other things. The reason we are to put those days behind us is because too much reminiscing over how great we were can cause pride to rise up and distract us from our calling now.

LAW SCHOOL

From the time I was 12, I dreamt of being a lawyer and talked about it for most of my younger years. At the age of 35, I applied to law school, took the Law Students Admissions Test (LSAT), did fairly well, and got into a law program. In the beginning, I could see myself as a practicing high-power attorney, helping the poor and getting paid well. I came into agreement with pride, thinking that *I* could do this and *I* would be successful, et cetera.

My first semester in law school was fair, but I flunked my second semester. I went up before the school board for review. They were to decide whether I would stay in school or be placed on a probationary period at worst. To my dismay, they told me that I was not cut out for law school or for being a lawyer. It was humiliating and embarrassing, to say the least, being kicked out by the program. I had people ask me how my grades were, and I had to tell them I was no longer a law student.

The whole ordeal was disillusioning, and there was a grieving deep in my spirit. I knew that I was destined to go to law school and get my degree. However, like Joseph's dream of his future, this rending process—pursing my lifelong dream only to fail—is what God used to break me of anything that had "I" in it. Previously when I was in school, I had bragged on *myself* getting the good grades, *me* pushing forward for my dream, and *me* getting all the glory. It was time for me to lay law school on God's altar. I told Him that I would do it only if He wanted me to. In addition, if I did do it, it would be according to His will only, not mine. Before my destiny could begin to unfold, I needed to get to the end of my own strength and let Him perform through me, relying on His strength.

From Bottom to Top

A year later, I applied to another law school and ended up in the top 25 percent of the class. The state bar, where the law school resided, required each first year student from my program to take an exam, also known as the "baby bar" exam, in order to receive credit for the first year. The state bar tested over 800 students from other law schools who had finished their first year at that time. Less than 27 percent of those who took it passed. When I took the exam I was scared, but I continued to give God the glory and honor. I told Him that I could not be a law student without His working through me and I was totally dependent on Him. After I received the results, I was shaking!

I was in the top 10 percent of over 800 law students. When I was operating in pride, I had flunked out of law school. However, when I operated outside of pride in brokenness and humility, I leaned on God and found His grades were much better than I had dreamed.

Pride will lead us into the lie that we know how to do things better than God—the same lie that Eve believed when she ate the apple. She followed the advice of satan and was deceived. Likewise, I believed that I was able to get through law school alone, and the experience of that deception cost me. A whole year was spent working toward nothing because it was in my flesh. It is pride which says, "I know better than God knows" about what I should do.

"WHO DOES SHE THINK SHE IS?"

Pride also states that we are better than other people in certain talents, gifts of the Spirit, and relationship roles. Pride makes us look at another sister and think that she is not as "spiritual" as we are. In other words, it makes us think more highly of ourselves than we should. As I discussed earlier in my story, pride keeps women from feeling as though they are accepted by another group of women. Pride tells those who are unaccepted that they are not good enough for us and we are better than they are and we don't want them in our group. Pride says, "Thank You, God, that I'm not like that fallen sister." Pride says, "Why did they pick her to do that task when I'm better?" Pride says, "How can that woman treat her children and husband like that?" Pride says, "Who does she think she is?"

Pride is always questioning God's purpose and plan for others' lives and even our own, and it enables us to think that we can make it alone without God. It tells us that we know how to plan our life, our children's lives, and our husband's. It is pride that says to us that our husband should be doing things another way at work and that our children do not measure up to what we would want them to be, even though they are fearfully and wonderfully made by God Himself.

THE FALL FROM HEAVEN

It was actually pride in satan's heart that caused him to fall from Heaven.

> *All your pomp has been brought down to the grave, along with the noise of your harps; maggots are spread out beneath you and worms cover you. How you have fallen from Heaven, O morning star, son of the dawn! You have been cast down to the earth, you who once laid low the nations! You said in your heart, "I will ascend to Heaven; I will raise my throne above the stars of God; I will sit enthroned on the mount of assembly, on the utmost heights of the sacred mountain"* (Isaiah 14:11-13 NIV).

Satan must have been in an incredible position prior to his fall, because he would have never tried to usurp God had he been in a low position. A person does not see a new employee coming into a huge company and trying to get the chief executive officer's (CEO's) position on the first day. Usually the person that is bucking for the CEO's position is someone that is very near to him already.

Likewise, the more we grow in Christ and actually see ourselves becoming more like Him, the easier it might be to pat ourselves on the back. All of a sudden, we turn around and people want our prayers, our counsel, our leadership, and so on. We start at a low place, and as we grow spiritually we go higher due to our increased knowledge of God. However, it is that very increased knowledge of God that can actually bring us down if it is not used correctly. The trouble with pride is that it is deceptive.

We might say, "I would never allow pride to enter me." But the very fact that we've said this is prideful, because we are saying that we are strong enough to resist the spirit of pride alone. It is only by God's grace that we are kept from the spirit of pride. The way to combat the spirit of pride is by the spirit of the fear of the Lord, which I will discuss more in a later book. Therefore, in order to stay free from the spirit of pride and its presence in our life, it is necessary to walk in a true fear of the Lord.

"I Am Weak!"

It is our natural leaning to "boast" because the Lord gives us joy and encouragement as fruits and gifts of the spirit (see Gal. 5:22-23; Rom. 12:8 NIV). The combination of these two bends us to a "boasting" which is natural for our spirit walk. If God created us as such creatures, then what are we to boast in? God wants us boasting in our weaknesses, not our strengths. Paul demonstrates this in his letter to the Corinthians when he writes that he himself had great revelation from the Lord and even went up into the third heaven. However, he doesn't go around telling everyone of his great revelations and how the Lord used him. Instead, he boasts about his weaknesses, and when he boasts in them he is made strong.

> *Of such an one will I glory: yet of myself I will not glory, but in mine infirmities. For though I would desire to glory, I shall not be a fool; for I will say the truth: but now I forbear, lest any man should think of me above that which he seeth me to be, or that he heareth of me* (2 Corinthians 12:5-6 KJV).

Paul states that if he is to boast in *anything* in himself it will be his weaknesses, not his strengths. If he is to boast about *anything* good, it is to be of God. Paul was greatly used by God—more than the other apostles were—and tells the sufferings he went through in Second Corinthians 11. However, he continually exclaimed that he is the least of all the apostles, and prior to his actual death he described himself as the chief of sinners in Colossians.

Paul goes on to talk about his "thorn in the flesh," which was sent as a messenger of satan to torment him. When he pleaded with God to remove the thorn, God's response was that His grace was sufficient.

> *But He said to me, "My grace is sufficient for you, for My power is made perfect in weakness"* (2 Corinthians 12:9 NIV).

Paul states that this was allowed in order to keep him from becoming conceited because of all the revelation he had received from the Father. He discovered that although the tormenting thorn in the flesh was not removed by God, His grace was sufficient for overcoming it. If God allowed Paul to have a "thorn in the flesh," the reason was that He did not want pride to enter Paul's heart. Likewise, we cannot allow pride to enter our hearts.

I Prayed That In

Are we busy telling people what we've prayed in, what we've put together, what ministry we helped out with our gifts, or what person we mentored?

> *But when you pray, go into your room, close the door and pray*
> *to your Father, who is unseen. Then your Father, who sees what*
> *is done in secret, will reward you* (Matthew 6:6 NIV).

If we are doing that, my sister, we are boasting in ourselves and are committing the sin of pride. What we should be boasting about is how much we would foul it up if it were dependent on us. We should also boast about the Holy Spirit's work in us, and in doing so, leave out the word "me."

For example, when a person interceding for something miraculous discovers that it has happened, they should not boast about it. Instead, they should keep their mouth closed and let God get *all* the glory. People can be deceived in this arena and believe that they are allowing themselves to be a testimony of God's work. In order to know the right time to testify, we need to ask ourselves, "Did the Holy Spirit prompt me to say this?" If the answer is no, then it is our flesh rising up, not God's glory. Am I receiving the applause of people when I'm giving a testimony, or is the Lord receiving all the glory? God receives *all* the glory for everything He does, and when we try to let others know of our hand in helping God on earth, most of the time it is a pride issue.

Broken for Christ

In 2004, I personally experienced a season of being broken of pride. I prayed for humility at that time and received it. Just a word of counsel— when you pray for humility it does not always happen in the closet; at times, it's a public breaking. After the prayer the following week, a certain public circumstance happened that made me wish that the Rapture would happen within the hour. Out of past sinful behavior, I had brought a humble breaking to my doorstep. Many people were upset with me and wanted to see less of me. They even met to agree that I was to be loathed by the entire world for my horrible sinful behavior and, as a result, felt as though it was their duty to let me know how much they loathed me. I was crushed, embarrassed, depressed, disheartened, and broken, to say the least. You name every negative emotion you can think of and chances are, I felt it. Although while it was happening I felt like I wanted to die, what I didn't know was that God would use that to catapult me out of bondage, and He would stir up my desire for the spirit of the fear of the Lord.

NEW WORLD

I became a student of the fear of the Lord and began pouring myself into finding out more about this Spirit of God. I came to understand who God was and what my posture was to be toward His Word. I then yielded myself to the Great Physician's table and allowed Him to take pride out of my heart. I became new again in a way that is indescribable.

The world looked different than it had prior to this event. Before, things had seemed so routine and ordinary to me. However, after my breaking experience, I had a deeper revelation of God's greatness on this earth, and He poured His sustaining grace and mercy on me daily, allowing me to live. I trembled at the thought of how I had offended Him in the past and how much I had done to defy Him and His Word. Through my disobedience, I had mocked Him to His face. I got on my face and repented for my sins, especially the sin of rebellion through pride, and asked for His grace to empower me in fighting against it.

A REPENTANT HEART

Today, I keep myself in a posture of repentance each day, seeking to maintain a repentant heart and asking God to keep me "low." Heidi Baker is an example of a humble heart at work in the Kingdom. Heidi Baker is a missionary in Africa and has many churches and has taken on adopting many children as her own. She is one of the most humble people I have ever met. When I first came across Heidi in 2004, the Lord gave me a vision of me with my short blonde hair in a taupe suit bending over on the floor of a stage in a church praying. I had very short hair at this time and it could not be platinum enough because I was going through a phase that I wanted to be stripped of all vanity. In the midst of this season, the Lord then told me to find out about Heidi Baker, so I did a search on the Internet and came across a Web page that had several of her videos. I randomly picked out a video to watch, and in that video Heidi Baker had short blonde hair and was in a taupe suit bent over on a stage singing in tongues. It was the very vision God had given me. The Holy Spirit quickened me to learn from her life the humility that she has walked in as a missionary in Africa. I desire humility like her. God says that He dwells in those who have a contrite and lowly (humble) spirit.

> *For thus saith the high and lofty One that inhabiteth eternity, whose name is Holy; I dwell in the high and holy place, with him also that is of a contrite and humble spirit, to revive the spirit of the humble, and to revive the heart of the contrite ones* (Isaiah 57:15 KJV).

Webster's defines "contrite" as "feeling deep sorrow or remorse for having sinned or done wrong; penitent; showing a result for remorse or guilt." We need to stay contrite; it keeps our hearts repentant toward God. David demonstrates this position so well in Psalms.

> *Have mercy upon me, O God, according to Thy lovingkindness: according unto the multitude of Thy tender mercies blot out my transgressions. Wash me thoroughly from mine iniquity, and cleanse me from my sin. For I acknowledge my transgressions: and my sin is ever before me. Against Thee, Thee only, have I sinned, and done this evil in Thy sight: that Thou mightest be justified when Thou speakest, and be clear when Thou judgest. Behold, I was shapen in iniquity; and in sin did my mother conceive me. Behold, Thou desirest truth in the inward parts: and in the hidden part Thou shalt make me to know wisdom. Purge me with hyssop, and I shall be clean: wash me, and I*

*shall be whiter than snow. Make me to hear joy and gladness; that the bones which Thou hast broken may rejoice. Hide Thy face from my sins, and blot out all mine iniquities. Create in me a clean heart, O God; and renew a right spirit within me. Cast me not away from Thy presence; and take not Thy Holy Spirit from me. Restore unto me the joy of Thy salvation; and uphold me with Thy free Spirit. Then will I teach transgressors Thy ways; and sinners shall be converted unto Thee. Deliver me from bloodguiltiness, O God, Thou God of my salvation: and my tongue shall sing aloud of Thy righteousness. O Lord, open Thou my lips; and my mouth shall shew forth Thy praise. For Thou desirest not sacrifice; else would I give it: Thou delightest not in burnt offering. **The sacrifices of God are a broken spirit: a broken and a contrite heart**, O God, Thou wilt not despise. Do good in Thy good pleasure unto Zion: build Thou the walls of Jerusalem. Then shalt Thou be pleased with the sacrifices of righteousness, with burnt offering and whole burnt offering: then shall they offer bullocks upon Thine altar* (Psalm 51 KJV).

David is penitent for his sins and boasts about his weaknesses and God's strengths. He describes that which God desires—a broken and contrite heart. This is a position that is difficult to stay in, particularly in the western world. Our culture thrives on self-dependence and being "strong." However, if the truth be known, we are all wretched and naked before the Lord in filthy rags (see Isa. 64:6). I pray daily to be broken and contrite. If a person is hesitant about praying this position of dependence then they are in rebellion, because this is what God desires out of each and every one of His children. Who among us is willing to have a contrite heart? God uses those who have a contrite heart, such as King David, Joseph, Moses, Paul, Esther, Ruth, and others.

How Low Can You Go?

We also have to stay "low," or humble. Webster's defines "low" as, "of little height or elevation; not high or tall." My favorite visual aid for lowness is given by Jesus in the book of Luke, describing dining at a wedding feast.

When someone invites you to a wedding feast, do not take the place of honor, for a person more distinguished than you may have been invited. If so, the host who invited both of you will come and say to you, "Give this man your seat." Then, humiliated, you will have to take the least important place. But when you are invited, take the lowest place, so that when your host comes, he will say to you, "Friend, move up to a better place." Then you will be honored in the presence of all your fellow guests (Luke 14:8-10 NIV).

Jesus speaks of maintaining a position of humility by humbling ourselves and staying "low," so that in the appropriate time we will be exalted. This is not done by always appearing humble; sometimes a humble person is actually bold. Instead, this is a position of knowing who we are in Christ and that without Him we are *nothing*.

If we do not allow pride to come in and exalt us, then with our God-given humility—humbling ourselves and yielding to Him—we will find that while maintaining a posture of humility, we will actually be brought forward. I have good news about being brought forward. Remember earlier when I said that God's chastening is often in public, not in the closet? He also elevates us in public and not in the closet.

For example, in 2006 I received a dream from the Lord where I was going to go through great persecution from other Christians. In the dream the people were very tall. I was walking around and heard them all clamoring to talk with a specific couple, Mr. and Mrs. Pride. Then we all went into a larger room to listen to a well-known teacher of the Word of God. In this room I sat by another lady whom I had known years earlier somewhere else. This lady had been treated as an outcast by her church because her husband had cheated on her and left. While I was sitting by this lady, a partition came down between me and all of the tall people who were sitting by Mr. and Mrs. Pride, and I was no longer able to be a part of them. After that, a lady in the dream came up to me and said that I had two demons on me, and I told her that I did not. Then I walked away dejected in the dream for a long walk and eventually came back to tell her I did not have two demons on me. She apologized to me, said that she knew and was sorry, and the dream was over.

I had no clue what I was in for when I had this dream. I told Rich, my husband, about my dream, and he could not believe the people that were rejecting me in the dream and the fact that I even had it. I even repented to God for having the dream. However, things turned around within two weeks while my husband and I were sitting together that the very dream and people I dreamed about were doing to me exactly what was in the dream. Some people treated me as an outcast, as though I was a Jezebel. However, God prepared me for this attack of the enemy against my reputation and I knew that I had to trust Him that in the end those people would know the truth and He would elevate me in front of them.

This season of walking out the misunderstanding of others lasted nearly two years. Doors that once had been opened for me to minister were now shut and I was being watched like a hawk by different people as though I was a false prophet who had to be stopped. Rich and I knew the truth and had to continue to trust God through this season, knowing that there was a purpose in it.

Eventually, the very people that treated me like that later came to me and apologized and told me that they had been deceived by the devil regarding the way they perceived me.

Then before I knew God had elevated me in front of them where bigger doors for ministry opened up and I was again received back into the group to minister, as well. However, this time when I ministered the anointing on my life was stronger. I had walked through such a great persecution just by simply loving God and going after Him with all that was within me. I was an abandoned lover of Jesus and did not care if people thought my love was not of God. However, those who had persecuted me saw that in their wrong judgments against me, they had come against a prophet who loved her Jesus, and they were cut to the core by the Sword of the Lord. (see Hebrews 4:12). The Holy Spirit revealed their motives and intentions to them and they repented. I had to be patient and wait and not turn against them or defend myself so that the Lord would in due time exalt me.

When God elevates us, others see us coming forward wherever He may have us. We need to guard against wanting people to know that we prayed for something. Do not testify of God-given gifts without the Holy Spirit's prompting. Keep from "one-upping" others. "One-upping" is when someone tells us something and instead of meditating on how good God was in that circumstance we say, "Well, God did *this* for me...." Then we take the attention off of the work of the Holy Spirit in another's life and bring it to ourselves.

SELF-AMBITION VERSUS GOD-AMBITION

Pride is a constant battle in America because we are all about self-ambition, our reputation, and our status. When we begin to go through a breaking, we might find ourselves wanting to make excuses to those who are observing our breaking, explaining why things are the way they are. Paul states that we are to boast in our weaknesses, so that in that "boasting" God will make us strong.

That is exactly what He did for me after that intense humbling I experienced earlier. The people that loathed me and had come against me before were the very ones who God elevated me in front of when the right time came. Those people judged me and condemned me as a horrible person. However, God showed His mercy through my weakness by delivering me from bondages and was able to receive all the glory for the miracle in my life. In addition, some of these people now ask me for advice. That is something I would have never foreseen in the midst of trials.

Prideful Behaviors

QUESTIONS:

1. Is there any area in which you have allowed pride to operate?

2. Do you want the spotlight or others to know what incredible things you are doing? If so, is there pride in it?

3. Do you see other sisters as beneath you or think that you are better than they are?

4. What Scriptures can you confess in order to maintain a position of humility?

8

Judging Others

S isters refrain from judging each other because they love each other. This is an easy ensnarement of the enemy because we somehow only think of the "big judgments" we make against our sisters, and we tend to overlook the "little judgments" we make everyday. With God, there is no degree of sin. Sin is sin, and whether or not the judgment is "big" or "small," it is still sin. What does God's Word tell us about judging others?

> *Humble yourselves before the Lord, and He will lift you up. Brothers, do not slander one another. Anyone who speaks against his brother or judges him speaks against the law and judges it. When you judge the law, you are not keeping it, but sitting in judgment on it. There is only one Lawgiver and Judge, the One who is able to save and destroy. But you—who are you to judge your neighbor?* (James 4:10-12 NIV)

The Holy Spirit gave me a song ten years ago regarding judgment so that I could share it with others and help them understand the severity of it. The words are:

Verse 1:

*We are born in this America
with so much freedom given here,
yet we see faces stricken
with pain, sorrow, and fear
caused by simple judgments,
needlessly made in vain,
and I hear the Savior whisper,
"Child, tell them who I am."*

Chorus:

*Why do you judge them? Do you have the power to save?
Was it you who died on the Cross and rose from the grave?
Look to the Savior and follow in His path.
Put aside your judgments and share the love He has.*

Verse 2:

*Is that your sister crying?
Did you cause her tears to fall?
Is that your brother on his knees,
no longer standing tall?
Tell me who did this;
who brought about this pain?
Tell them to look to Jesus
and call upon His name.*

Chorus

Verse 3:

*He has so much love.
You can hear the angels singing
hallelujahs from above,
and His voice trumpets down.*

You are all God's children;
spread His love all around.

Chorus

"Put aside your judgments and share the love He has." What God wants us to do is to put aside all of our judgments. There are so many times that I have caught myself thinking about what another sister could do to be a better leader, wife, or mentor. However, the Holy Spirit revealed to me that I was judging her. I was asking Him, "What, how is that judgment, God?" The Holy Spirit showed me that when I said these things, instead of being a true sister and interceding for what appeared to be ungodly, I was cursing her and making judgments about her. I repented immediately and put all my little judgments under the blood.

LITTLE FOXES THAT SPOIL THE VINE

God's Word says that it is *"the little foxes that spoil the vines"* (Song of Sol. 2:15). Satan is not going to come at us with an obvious, blatant sin of judging another. Instead, he brings us to a place where we look at a situation and determine that we know how that sister should act. We are not covering her with our prayer, as we should.

I have heard John Bevere, at different churches, say that the reason Christ could judge the Pharisees and Sanhedrin was because He was willing to die for them. This goes back to the words in the song. Only He who was nailed to the Cross, died for their sins, and rose from the grave is the One who can pass judgment. Are we willing to die for our sister when we are passing judgment on her? Are we allowing pride to creep in and make us feel better?

Unless we are willing to lay down our lives and truly love our sister, we cannot even think about judging her. Sometimes we can mean the right thing, but we go about doing it the wrong way. For example, we might know a sister and see that she is going down the wrong path, and we truly want to bring her the truth in love. Yet, if it is not said the right way, it can come across as judgment. Therefore, it is necessary to wait upon the Lord's timing and ask His Holy Spirit to guide us and possess us so that we can be a vessel of love to our sister and bring correction or teaching. For example, I am mentoring a young lady now who has backslidden from the Lord, and the Holy Spirit is wooing her back. It would turn her away from God if I was to confront her about her ungodly behavior now because she will feel judged and flogged.

SPLINTERS AND LOGS

How do we correct? Jesus states that we are not to pull the sawdust out of someone else's eye until we get the log out of our own.

> *Why do you look at the speck of sawdust in your brother's eye and pay no attention to the plank in your own eye? How can you say to your brother, "Brother, let me take the speck out of your eye," when you yourself fail to see the plank in your own eye? You hypocrite, first take the plank out of your eye, and then you will see clearly to remove the speck from your brother's eye* (Luke 6:41-42 NIV).

As we look at an area of sin in another sister, we need to examine our own history for that same sin and see where our plank lies. I hope that it will be floating down the river and out of our eyes.

You may find, as you examine yourself in the same area, that you, too, are dealing with this sin in some fashion. If this is the case, there needs to be repentance and turning from the sin and asking God to help you walk in righteousness and right standing. It is after you have examined your own sin that you can go to your sister who has the splinter in her eye. In love, you can give her your testimony in regards to pulling this plank out of your eye. After the testimony, the sister might *allow you* to look at the sawdust in her eye and assist in getting it out.

If, on the other hand, the plank is floating down the river from past removal (which would be the most desired case), then seek God's word for the sister who has a splinter. When an eye surgeon operates on a patient's eye, he first has the patient tell him the problem they have been experiencing before they allow him to operate. Therefore, when we go to pull the sawdust out of a sister's eye we have to be guided by the Holy Spirit. We allow the Holy Spirit to prompt her to come to us, or we go to her if she regularly volunteers to seek information from us (if there is a mentor relationship). Removing the speck in her eye is possible when done in this manner. For example, one lady I mentor talks about sex topics a lot. She feels as though she is the expert in this area and tries to push her opinions off on others and looks for opportunities to introduce this subject. Initially, I would listen to her discuss different occasions where she had spoken about the topic of sex yet again in an inappropriate place in public. Finally, the Holy Spirit gave me the green light (the opportunity) where I could address this issue with the lady. I looked at her and said, "You know, you sure do talk about sexual things a lot, and I don't think this is God but rather a stronghold you have." She received it well and we were able to work through it and help her. However, it was only because we had the relationship before I said this that she was able to receive it.

A CHANGE OF CLOTHES

For example, if we have a sister who dresses unseemly in church and draws attention to herself in a way that is not holy, we should seek the Holy Spirit's counsel. If God wants us to deal with the situation, we will not be agitated or frustrated with this immature sister. Rather, we will feel compassion and a desire to cover her for her own sake, not for our sake. We will find ourselves moved deeply for her to experience the fullness of God's love, and we will be a vessel of love in the process.

After His love possesses us, our conversation might sound something like this: "Mary, you are an attractive girl and God has blessed you with beauty. You know, God really shines in you when you wear things that are so becoming to you while also covering the parts of you that He only wants revealed to your husband. When I was a new Christian, I had to make that transformation in my wardrobe. May I share what God revealed to me?"

Some women may find this offensive merely reading it. However, when

God's Holy Spirit possesses us there should not be offense, because the motive is love. Actually, many times people are screaming deep down for someone to come help them. Remember, God is love and our motive should be out of love. If it is done in love then God's Holy Spirit will prepare the other sister's heart in order that she will receive, and then she will willingly lay herself down on the table for us to pull the sawdust out of her eye by His Holy Spirit. She will ask us, "What kind of dress is godly?"

Sometimes it might not be this gentle and God's will is an actual rebuke. Remember, although correction needs to come, His motive is out of love for His children. A rebuke usually comes after someone has received the truth but then turns away in error. For example, the rebuke might come after having talked with Mary, who dresses in a godly fashion for a while, but then reverts to her lifestyle of provocative dressing. At this point, she does so with the knowledge that it is sinful and is a stumbling block to others. Allow the Holy Spirit to move in the right time to bring about the rebuke. It might sound like this: "Mary, I don't know if you remember our discussion earlier about your dressing this way. Well, I bring that up because I believed that you understood that this type of dressing was ungodly and did not bring glory to God. What you should know is that when we first talked you may have truly been ignorant of it. However, after being fully informed about the way to walk in this area, if you continue to go against it, you do so willfully and there is no sacrifice for that sin (see Heb. 10:26). If you continue to dress like this, you are willfully sinning against God and are walking in disobedience and rebellion to His Word. He requires us to be holy because He is holy. Do you think that this dress is a good representation of God to the world?" I hope that she will answer no and take the rebuke in love because that is the motive—not judgment. When I confronted the woman who talked about sex a lot, I had the green light, the opportunity, to discuss something in a manner that was ungodly. The Holy Spirit brought it to her attention to where she knew it was a sin to talk about perverse things.

"IF SOMEONE DOESN'T SAY IT, THEN I WILL"

Judgment is a difficult ensnarement to recognize among women because, to be honest, sometimes women are more honest than they should be. Have you heard, "Oh, I have to be honest with her," or "If someone doesn't say anything to her, then I will"? This is not of God and is not only judgment, but pride as well; it will actually bring one into the same position as the sister they are judging. The Word teaches not to judge, unless you want to be judged.

> *You, therefore, have no excuse, you who pass judgment on someone else, for at whatever point you judge the other, you are condemning yourself, because you who pass judgment do the same things. Now we know that God's judgment against those who do such things is based on truth. So when you, a mere man, pass judgment on them and yet do the same things, do you think you will escape God's judgment?* (Romans 2:1-3 NIV)

If we judge another sister in the area of sin we detest in her, we can expect to fall into that same sin if not worse.

Since 2001, my family has had no cable television in our home. We only watch movies we have bought since we do not watch television. My husband and I are now very careful regarding the movies we let our two boys watch, because the Holy Spirit revealed to us the enemy's plot to reach our boys through movies that we would normally not consider bad. We watch out for anything with witchcraft, spells, and the like. In addition, we watch the movies' content and the different ratings regulated by the licensing agency.

I found myself in a situation where I knew another mother had some movies that I didn't allow my sons to watch. I was almost shocked and even discussed this serious error in her decisions with my husband. (I'm showing my arrogance here, but I've repented.) I talked at some length about how she was deceived and uninformed.

A few weeks later, my eldest son, who is a huge skateboarder, wanted to watch a movie at the theaters. I was in the midst of preparing for my second year of law school finals, and I was very depleted and stressed to the max. Prior to the release of this movie, I had adamantly told him time after time that he would not be viewing it. Weeks later, however, during this time of stress and vulnerability, I found myself considering it. What was wrong with me? I, who am so adamant and strict with my children, keeping them from all things that I would consider ungodly, was acting out of character.

I asked my husband what was wrong with me. I was going through a trial that I had brought on myself. The root of it was not lust of the world, because that root had already been dug out a couple of years earlier. Instead, this seething attack almost felt as though I was being seduced into making unholy decisions. Praise God that He showed me the problem, and I was immediately given direction by the Holy Spirit to repent of my earlier judgment on that mother. He showed me that His grace had kept me, lest I forget. I then in turn prayed for her and her restoration in this area. The attack stopped as soon as I had made that confession, repented, and turned to pray for her situation.

UNNECESSARY TRIBULATION

Many times when I'm experiencing a trial or tribulation, my initial reaction is to ask God if I have judged anyone wrongfully. He will show me that many times I have. I immediately put it under the blood and ask for forgiveness for judging that person, and He restores me. There have been occasions where I found myself acting in a manner that is totally out of character. Usually in those times it is one of two things. The first is I may still have sinful behavior that needs to be rooted out of me. The second is I may have judged another person. We need to examine our life and find out if we are judging someone.

In addition, I always bless those whom I find out I've judged and cancel any type of curses I might have spoken against them. Curses are not swear words, as the world views cursing, but are words that do not speak life but death. Remember that life and death are in the power of the tongue, and if we are speaking judgments we are speaking death, not life.

> Out of the same mouth come praise and cursing. My brothers, this should not be. Can both fresh water and salt water flow from the same spring? My brothers, can a fig tree bear olives, or a grapevine bear figs? Neither can a salt spring produce fresh water (James 3:10-12 NIV).

Judge Not

QUESTIONS:

1. Have you judged others?

2. Are you associating with other people who judge others?

3. Are you watching television shows or reading magazines that judge others?

4. Are you undergoing any tribulations or trials that could be contributed to judging others?

5. What Scriptures can you confess in order to have love toward others instead of judging them?

9

Covetous Jealousy

You shall not covet your neighbor's house. You shall not covet your neighbor's wife, or his manservant or maidservant, his ox or donkey, or anything that belongs to your neighbor (Exodus 20:17 NIV).

Sisters do not covet what another sister has. This area is a weakness among women because the enemy uses it to make women feel as though they got "short-changed." So many areas need to be discussed here to bring freedom and unity among women. I must caution everyone that I'm giving an opportunity to leave this book for a moment because we are tackling a heavy subject. After returning, we will get started on a subject that is highly overlooked and swept under the carpet. What we will do is get into the dark area of covetous jealousy and the results of this sin.

THE WRONG JEALOUSY

First, there are two types of jealousy, not one, although many people only see one type of jealousy. However, I know by experience and by God's Holy

Spirit that there are two, having been delivered from wounded-trespassed jealousy and healed of it. We will be discussing "covetous jealousy" at this point. Later, for those women who need deliverance from the other, there is a discussion on the subject of "trespassed jealousy" in the third book of this series. I encourage people to read that section if they need healing and deliverance from "wounded-trespassed jealousy."

All right, women, let's get started. The enemy often sets up circumstances to make one sister jealous of the other through coveting. Again, there are two types of jealousy, "covetous jealousy" and "trespassed jealousy." The first one, "covetous jealousy," is described in the Ten Commandments: "You shall not covet" (see Exod. 20:17). Jealousy results when we desire that which someone else owns. "Trespassed jealousy" is where someone else has coveted something of ours, and we are aware of that covetousness. It puts us in fear that we will lose what is ours and that the other person will get it.

First, I would like to distinguish between sharing and coveting. Webster's Dictionary defines "share" as "to receive, use, experience enjoy, endure in common with another or others." Something that we share with others is generally viewed as common or public property. Library books sort of fall into this category, at least, people who do not return them seem to think so. Also, you might have teaching audios that you share with others. Distinguishable from sharing is "coveting." Webster's defines this as "to long for with envy."

PRIDE, LUST, AND SELFISHNESS

Covetous jealousy is rooted in pride of life, lust of the flesh, and selfishness. As seen in the Ten Commandments, we first covet by desiring a person's actual property (jewelry, clothes, etc.), desiring a person's relationships (husband, friendships, children, etc.) or desiring a person's status (position of leadership, job, ministry, etc.). As we discussed earlier, pride says that we are better than our sisters, and because we are better we should have the best—even if we don't own it and our sister does. There is also lust. Lust says, "I like the way that jewelry looks on her and I want it; I like the way her husband looks and acts, and I would like a man like him; I like the position that she has in the church and I want that." Selfishness says *I* want that, *I* should be doing that, and *I* should have a husband like that.

ME CASA NO ES TU CASA
(MY HOUSE IS NOT YOUR HOUSE)

This is a *serious* sin, because in this case one does not sin in a vacuum. It affects not only the sinner but the other sister and her family as well, especially in the area of relationships and *most* of all with *husbands!*

Let's deal with personal property first. *"You shall not covet your neighbor's house"* is the first part of the commandment not to covet (see Exod. 20:17). This is in regard to "property." Homes, jewelry, and clothes are a big issue with women in this area. If we are asking a sister to borrow her jewelry or making comments about how we like another sister's jewelry or clothes—which would make her feel uncomfortable—then we are in a place of coveting them. What we should be doing is thinking of how nice that jewelry looks on that sister—not on us.

If we are giving a sister's property more than a first look and are eyeing it with desire, then we are probably coveting. We need to confess our sin and put it under the blood. Repenting, we ask God to help us see our sister as an honorable vessel and to take away anything in us that is of the world. The world covets and desires what other people have. There is a famous saying: "We are trying to keep up with the Joneses." That is an attitude of coveting established in the world. It's saying that our personal property is not good enough and we are being ungrateful for that which God has blessed us with. We are being spoiled and have not thanked our Father for what He has given us. This is especially true in homes, cars, and big-ticket items. What we need is to become grateful and thank the Father all the time.

A PINK ICE NECKLACE

I have a very inexpensive necklace that cost me only four dollars. It looks like a pink ice stone on a small line choker. When I wore it to church one day,

I had a friend tell me that she loved pink ice and she loved my necklace and really wanted one like it and if I died I should will it to her. Although this friend is a good friend and it was said in jest, I felt uncomfortable. Later, the Holy Spirit gave me revelation that what this sister was doing was coveting my possession. Usually, we think the good Christian thing to do is to let our friends borrow our jewelry, clothes, or other items. However, what this is doing instead is enabling their sin of coveting.

I experienced this form of coveting in my own life after my husband and I had been working on our home for a couple of years. We had transformed it with the dramatic flair of many different countries. I was so pleased with the work that we did on the house. People would stop by and discuss how beautiful the house looked, saying that I should seriously consider going into interior decorating. This swelled my ego. Later on, I found out from a friend that another woman had been decorating her home. My friend also ranted and raved about how incredible it was. I was somewhat taken aback and thought that in the price range, we had the best home for the buck.

I later found myself driving by the house trying to look through the shutters and even discussing the matter repeatedly with my husband. They had bigger-ticket items in the other home because they could afford things that I dreamt of having in my own home. I became obsessed with the other home and desired to compare it to ours to see which home truly was the best.

The Lord revealed that I was coveting the other home and actually being ungrateful for mine. I thought, "Lord, how could You say that? I *am* grateful." However, I discovered that I truly was coveting, and I had gotten so caught up in the situation that the rest of my life had stagnated because of my sin. I confessed this sin and repented, thanking God continuously for my own home. Before long, the other home was not an issue for me. Moreover, I was happy that the other family had such a nice home and was able to enjoy it.

COVETING BY NOT BEING OBEDIENT

If we have something the Lord has blessed us with, and then He asks us to give it to someone, we covet it if we are not obedient in giving it away. This can happen with offerings we are to give to the church, clothes, furniture, and so on. One thing I have learned is that I become restless if I'm not obedient to the Lord on this matter.

Recently, a friend gave me a brand new dress with the price tag still on it. It was very expensive and definitely my taste. However, when I got it the Lord told me to give it to a friend of mine, Pam. I was not obedient at first because I liked the dress a lot and desired to keep it. Besides, it was my style and it was even black, which is my favorite color in clothing. I wore it only one time. After that time, I kept seeing a vision of Pam in the dress. I could not bring myself to put it on again. I became restless until I gave the dress to Pam. Pam told me that she had recently had a birthday and her daughter had given her a bracelet. After receiving the bracelet from her daughter, Pam told the Lord that she would like a dress to go with the bracelet. Wouldn't you know that the dress I gave her from the Lord went perfectly with the bracelet?

It is like that any time we hold onto something in our possession that the Lord has asked us to give away. If we do not release it then we are coveting.

WESTERN BORROWING

This is a sensitive area because offense can easily creep up here if things are not said in love. We need to help our sister if she has a problem with coveting. We can do this by sharing with them the different ways that we have coveted which the Lord has shown to us. In America, coveting starts when we are in high school and we start sharing our clothes with our friends. Then we go to college, and before we know it we have to go to another girl's room to find our property.

This attitude is abundant in America because we promote it. We are more satisfied at that age and we feel good if we have everything we want, regardless of whether it is someone else's. If a teenage girl does not lend her clothes to her friends she will almost find them offended at her. What we need to do is begin teaching our daughters that this is coveting and use it as a teaching opportunity. We then need to be teachers for those in the Christian community as well as nonbelievers. God wants us to be grateful for what we have.

CHRISTMAS TOYS

Imagine two children, one is grateful and the other ungrateful. When Christmas comes, a mother gives the one that is grateful only one toy and the one less grateful a whole room full of toys. The ungrateful child says, "I wish that I had the toys the girl up the street has because her parents really gave her some nice things for Christmas." For the rest of the year, she returns from school each day talking about what every girl in her school got for Christmas. Not one "Thank you," or "I like what I received," is even peeped out of her mouth.

However, the one who is grateful and given only one toy ends up being so thankful that she desires to express it every day. Every day that she wakes up, she says, "I'm so thankful for that toy, Mom." Every day she returns home and states, "Mom, I really want to thank you for that toy; I feel so blessed." For the next year, all she says is how thankful she is. Which child will the mother desire to lavish upon the next Christmas? She will lavish upon the grateful child.

That is how God is with us. He wants to give *more* to those who are grateful. Those who steward their thankfulness toward Him and appreciate what they have been given receive more. Moreover, He wants to chasten the ungrateful to bring out a grateful heart in them.

When we see a sister who has something that we desire to wear or own, we need to thank God for her blessing but most of all thank Him for ours, too. This will not only bring about a grateful heart and break the bondage of coveting, but it will also bring great reward in our soul. As the Word says, the Lord prospers me as my soul prospers (see 3 John 1:2). If our soul is greatly prospering, then most likely our natural circumstances will be, as well.

A ONE-WOMAN MAN

Next, let's talk about relationships. *"You shall not covet your neighbor's wife"* is the second part of the commandment not to covet (see Exod. 20:17). It refers to coveting someone's relationships. This is an area where so much sin can be avoided if we put it under the blood quickly. I have found that many women need to know the boundaries for coveting other women's relationships.

First, let's talk about the most important one—the husband-wife relationship. This includes engaged persons as well. If a woman finds herself drawn to another woman's husband or fiancé, she should immediately seek God's grace to help her overcome. Scripture says that our mind is transformed by hearing the Word (see Romans 12:2). *"...What God has joined together, let not man separate,"* or should I say let not *woman* separate (Matt. 19:6). God's special design for earth and unity is found in marriage, and it is only in marriage where God has two people becoming one flesh. Much weight should be given to the sanctity of marriage.

Marriage is a place where one person can give themselves to the other, where nakedness is exposed, and where communion of the husband's and wife's souls takes place. This is a union that is so strong and such a threat to the enemy that he will stop at nothing to destroy it. It was the marriage unity between Adam and Eve that satan tried to destroy at the beginning of time. It is this unity that he tries to destroy between Jesus, our Bridegroom, and us, His Bride. Satan is after the marriage covenant. He is going to be forever unceasing at worming his way in to bring division. A house divided cannot stand, and he knows this (see Mark 3:25). At times, he does this through other willing vessels of covetous jealousy. It goes something like this.

THE PLAGUE?

Sitting in church, a woman finds herself looking across the aisle at another woman's husband. She notices how attractive he is and how he is so good to his wife. Before long, she desires to have a husband like that, and at times finds herself desiring someone "just like him." Then, when opportunity presents itself, she finds herself staring at him, and at different times, catching his eyes. Then, before she knows it, his wife has noticed this type of look from her and the couple is avoiding her like the plague. She tells herself that the wife is jealous and that she has done nothing wrong and is only trying to be nice.

This is covetous jealousy, and if this is what a woman is doing, it will cause another sister to be offended, experiencing trespassed jealousy—godly jealousy. Division could develop in the marriage if the couple gets into discussions about the woman's inappropriate looks toward the husband. What is worse, some women even go up to the man and start flirting with him. They call it sisterly love, but let me enlighten everyone that it is not sisterly love but *sin!*

I have reason for concern in this area because so many women are doing it. They are bringing division to another home and setting a seed of offense in the other sister's heart. When did it start to become covetous jealousy in the scenario above? When the woman took a second look at the man in church and continued. The first time she looked, it was temptation; the second time it was sin. She has crossed over from being tempted to sinning and the sin is covetous jealousy (see James 1:13-15). If this is happening to us, we need to confess it and repent. To repent means to change our mind toward that situation. We no longer will allow ourselves to look that way at married men or those that are engaged or even dating. Instead, we will seek the Lord for the right husband for us.

MORE THAN GROCERIES

My husband and I always go to the grocery store together. There was a woman that we found ourselves talking to often throughout our visits there. Believe me when I say that there was no possibility of threat. I knew there would be no concern of anything happening with my husband and this woman. However, one time when I didn't go with my husband to the store, he returned and stated that they had a good conversation. I didn't think anything about it. The next day, he told me that this woman said that she would like to have a husband "like him."

I could tell that my husband felt a little uncomfortable, although he didn't say it. When I first heard this, although I wasn't worried, I felt a check in my spirit. I didn't know what was going on. Later, when I sought an answer on this situation, the Holy Spirit revealed to me that this woman, although very innocent, was coveting my husband. Now, if I went up to her and asked what this was about, her wanting to marry my husband, she would think I had lost it! We don't see it like that, but we should. Although it's very innocent and is complementary to the man for being a good husband, underneath the enemy is pulling us more toward coveting him. If it continues, we will find ourselves doing more than telling him that we want a husband just like him.

FLIRTING

What we need to do—even those of us who are already married—is examine *any* area in our life where we might have been coveting the husband or relationship of another woman. We can see this even among friendships when couples become great friends. Before we know it, one wife might be joking with the other's husband and paying him inappropriate compliments. This behavior is considered flirting and should not be tolerated. We do not need to walk around with blinders on; we *do* need to use discernment in what is of the Lord and what is sin. We need to check our motives for saying something to another's husband. Is it because we want his attention or because we know it is of God? We need to search our heart motives.

Get this type of covetousness under the blood and pray to see all vessels as honorable vessels unto the Lord. Check the movies and shows that you are viewing on television, the magazines you are reading, and the group of women you are associating with. If you find out covetous jealousy is being condoned or encouraged among any of the things you are doing or people you are associating with, you need to make changes. Get into agreement with God's Word that such thoughts are not of God and are to be cast down immediately. Bring that stronghold down under the blood (see 2 Cor. 10:4). Remember that it is a choice, and choices are demonstrated not in thought alone but also in our actions. If we find ourselves wanting to compliment someone's husband, we need to ask ourselves if we would do it with Jesus standing there beside us. If we answer no, then we do not need to say it.

OLDER WOMEN WHO ARE EXAMPLES

I feel led to take a few moments here and speak to the elder women of the church. This is important because they are the ones who are examples to the younger women. Another form of flirting has been tolerated due to their age. It is assumed, due to the great number of years between older women and the younger husband of another woman, that it is all right to tell the husband that he is cute because they will not steal another woman's husband.

When I sought revelation on this, I discovered that it was still a form of covetousness, although one would hardly think so due to the age of the older woman. This area needs to be addressed because this is prominent among some older women. They see it as all right to tell younger women's husbands that they are cute. What do they receive out of it? A smile from the man, which is the result they are wanting. They are getting his attention. Is that a motive of love? Could it instead be self-seeking or even lust?

There is no doubt that older women sometimes get that butterfly feeling and desire relationship. We are in a human suit but we are more than that—we are spirit. Because we are spirit living in fleshly bodies, we need to ask ourselves if we are operating out of the spirit or flesh. I imagine Deborah, the judge from the Old Testament, and what she would have been like, and I cannot imagine her telling another woman's husband that he is cute.

If there is doubt, we need to ask if the Spirit of God told us to tell the man that he is cute. Jesus did nothing except for what He saw the Father doing.

> *Jesus gave them this answer: "I tell you the truth, the Son can do nothing by Himself; He can do only what He sees His Father doing, because whatever the Father does the Son also does"* (John 5:19 NIV).

That is what I would ask of all women. If a woman has any doubt the Spirit of God told her to tell the man he is cute or she would like a husband like him, then don't say it.

FRIENDSHIPS

Covetousness over relationships also happens when we desire other women's friendships or their relationships with their children. The enemy is most likely going to come at us through deception, and as it is said, deception is deceiving. One example is when there is a strong Christian woman in the church and we have an acquaintance or even good friend who is a close friend with that woman. Do we ever find ourselves saying, "I wish that strong Christian woman and I were good friends?" If we do, then we are most likely coveting the friendship of another. Instead, we should be joyful for the other sister's opportunity for relationship with the woman, because God is not without purpose. His purpose might be to build and strengthen her, while He might use a different relationship or circumstance to build and strengthen us.

I Want to Go Shopping

I experienced coveting a relationship with a good friend of mine who was a very close friend to a strong woman in the Lord. I envied their relationship because I didn't have as good a friendship with the woman as my friend did. I understood that they went out on many trips and spent a great deal of time together, and I knew that if she would get to know me, she would enjoy my company as well. I even discussed this with my husband who thought it a bit silly. Deep down I knew that it was wrong, but I strongly desired to get the same attention from the woman that my friend did. Eventually, I listened to the Holy Spirit and came to see that I was coveting something that was not mine. My friend had a good relationship with this woman, which was what I wanted. I repented and put it under the blood. After I did this, I actually laughed about how silly I had been over the whole situation.

Children's Personalities

Children have different personalities as well as different strengths and weaknesses. With one child, more prompting and encouraging might be needed to get them motivated to clean their room, whereas with another, merely a request to clean the room gets it done. What is the result of each method? The child's room gets cleaned. However, you don't use the same method in order to achieve the same result.

This is like God's dealings with us. With one sister, He might use a special relationship with a great Christian woman of God to mature her spiritual walk.

With another, He might use her husband. If both women have husbands who are not coming to church, God may be forming submissive wives out of each, but He might form submission in different methods to reach each husband. God might ask the one without the close friendship to be more submissive to her husband and not to question her husband's decisions because He is doing a work to bring the husband closer to Him. God's simple request turns her heart to do whatever He asks. On the other hand, the other woman who has the good friendship might be having difficulty hearing God because of the distractions in her life and her immaturity in the Lord. God sends her this great Christian woman whom she admires and they form a friendship. Out of the friendship comes mentoring and instruction that God desires to reach husbands, even through their wives' submissiveness. This woman is prompted and instructed in being a submissive wife. What is the result from both methods? God fashions a more submissive heart in each woman to reach her husband for His Kingdom. Are both methods the same? No. Is the result the same? Yes.

God has a purpose behind relationships that exist among women. Therefore, we are not to covet other's friendships. Instead, we are to praise God for the great friendships our sisters in Christ have. We are all a part of the sisterhood, and God has purpose behind each relationship we have with our sisters.

My mentor has many women whom she mentors. She spends quality time with each one according to God's plan. I am grateful for each of the women who spend time with her and love them as my own sisters. I do not get jealous of other women spending time with my mentor, but I encourage it and feel joyous for them. When my mentor tells me that she is taking a trip with one of the other women she mentors, I almost feel like jumping up and down for excitement. It's hard to explain, but I feel as though a gift is being given to my mentor and the other woman and it makes me feel joy for them.

THE REBELLIOUS CHILD AND OBEDIENT CHILD

Mothers should all desire godly relationships with their children. However, there are times when we might experience the trials and tribulations of raising children and find our child more rebellious than another mother's child. We find ourselves in the midst of adversity, staying on our knees in prayer, begging God to end this trial and bring our child closer to Him. In the midst of the storm, God is working. He might be working out many things. He might actually be working on making us bear more fruits of the Spirit. He might be working to root out more sin from our life. He might have us in the furnace with our child to refine both of us. God has a purpose and it is not without cause that we are going through something. Therefore rejoice with the mother whose child is serving the Lord, and be assured by His promises that your own child will soon be doing the same.

PICK ME!

Finally, we need to be sensitive in the area of coveting status. God ends the commandment by saying not to covet *anything that belongs to your neighbor,* which includes their status or position (see Exod. 20:17). This tends to begin as our desire to be more than we are. It crosses into coveting when we do not appreciate one woman's position of leadership and instead tend to frown on it or think that we could do a better job.

We need to be careful if we think that we are not at risk of committing this sin, because this temptation is more prevalent than we realize. It starts with something like this:

> *Oh, they got Jane to head up the women's ministry prayer group...that's good. I wonder who they considered for it. You know, she actually doesn't pray that much; I wonder why they would even consider her. In fact, I know Debra actually prays more than her, and for that matter, I do, too. Plus, I would actually be better for that position, and maybe I could even teach her a thing or two. I wonder if I should call her and offer her some of my expertise in praying.*

PROFANING YOUR SISTER

Another deception that lures us into coveting a woman's status or position appears contradictory to it—finding fault in her. This happens when we

117

befriend a woman because of her gift in the Lord, not simply because of her. We aren't seeking her friendship but her popularity. Later, we see flaws in her or become too familiar with her and literally do not honor her office in the five-fold ministry or gifts. Before we know it, we are taking her and her gift for granted and treating her as common. Jesus said that if we honor a prophet, we would get a prophet's reward.

> *Anyone who receives a prophet because he is a prophet will receive a prophet's reward, and anyone who receives a righteous man because he is a righteous man will receive a righteous man's reward* (Matthew 10:41 NIV).

We must stay sensitive to how we treat other women in leadership, even if they are friends. There are seasons when some women may be asked to step into leadership in the Kingdom's work. In these times, we must look to honor the woman as that office-holder and not just as a common friend—the reward we get will be a much higher one. If we honor the gift of God in her, we will get that reward. If we don't, then we will not receive that reward.

MAMA SHEILA'S OFFICE

For instance, my first mentor, Sheila, and I have formed a friendship. Although we are good friends and talked frequently during the years I was under her, I had to keep under the fear of the Lord. I did not want to take our relationship as common, but I honored her and the office she holds. She holds the office of a prophet and is used greatly to minister in many meetings. Being associated with her, I could have found myself desiring to be like her. I could have become too familiar and not honored the gift of God in her. If I had done either of these things, I would not have received the reward of a prophet. If I had tended in any way to dishonor her by saying something out of line, however slight, then I would not have received a prophet's reward. For example, when Elisha had trained under the prophet Elijah he served him. Because of his faithfulness and obedience to God to serve the prophet Elijah when it came time for Elijah to be promoted Elisha was given his mantel, he was promoted. I've noticed that when I honor prophets and other ministers of God, I receive a release in my destiny. God has a destiny for His daughters. Part of receiving the fullness of your destiny is honoring others. As we honor others, we receive more blessings from God. Doors open for us that no man can shut as we walk in obedience to God's will for our lives.

I praise God that teachings on the fear of the Lord are ingrained in me so strongly and that God has given me a respect for His anointed ones. It is ever so important that I continue in the fear of the Lord in order to ensure that I do not become too comfortable. If I become too comfortable then I might treat what is holy as common, thereby profaning it. I do not want to be irreverent to God's anointed ministers.

If we find ourselves desiring to be in the position of another woman or not honoring her as instructed by the Lord, then we might be coveting. We could be in rebellion as well as pride. If we have done this we need to confess and seek the guidance of God's Holy Spirit to expose the truth in the situation.

Covetous Jealousy

QUESTIONS:

1. Do you covet other people's personal possessions? If you do, what are they? Be specific.

2. Do you covet other women's friendships?

3. Do you covet other women's positions or status?

4. Do you covet other women's husbands?

5. Do you flirt with other women's husbands? If so, what do you need to change?

6. Do you covet other women's relationships with their children? If you do, what do you need to change about your relationship with your own children? Can you be more patient, longsuffering, forbearing, and so on?

7. Do you watch television shows or read books that demonstrate covetous jealousy? If so, what are they? Can you discipline yourself to stay away from these media?

8. Do you associate with other women who have covetous jealousy? If you do, pray about what the Lord wants you to do in regard to these relationships.

9. What Scriptures can you confess to keep pride out?

c h a p t e r

10

Offense

*A man's wisdom gives him patience; it is to his glory to overlook
an offense (*Proverbs 19:11 NIV).

The final thing sisters "don't do" that we need to discuss is the area
of offense. According to Webster's, "Offense" is defined as the act
of attacking or assaulting, bringing displeasure. Therefore, when we
are looking at an offense between sisters, it is something that has brought
displeasure or injury from one sister toward another sister.

For example, as I have been raising my oldest son, Christopher, and
watching the attack of the devil on his life, people have come to me and said,
well you must not have prayed enough or did not have good boundaries,
which is why your son is having struggles. They had no clue that I had
been doing a lot of prayer and that my husband and I had some very tight
boundaries, but in this season the enemy was attacking my son. It was not
because of us not praying enough, doing spiritual warfare enough. Their

123

immaturity in understanding what was happening to my son could have been an offense to me.

As we mature and grow more into the image of God, it is very likely that we will offend others as well as become offended by others many times over. Therefore, we need to dig deep into understanding what offense does and how we can turn it around to our good.

Working Offense to My Good

The Bible says that God works all things to our good (see Rom. 8:28). When we have an opportunity to be offended with someone we have to understand that God is going to use that offense to our good. God has revealed to me how offense can help conform us into the image of Christ.

To get the full revelation of what offense does in our lives, we need to look at an example of an opportunity for offense. As the Lord Jesus walked the earth, the following occurred between a group of people and a Canaanite woman:

> *Then the scribes and Pharisees who were from Jerusalem came to Jesus, saying, "Why do Your disciples transgress the tradition of the elders? For they do not wash their hands when they eat bread." He answered and said to them, "Why do you also transgress the commandment of God because of your tradition? For God commanded, saying, 'Honor your father and your mother'; and, 'He who curses father or mother, let him be put to death.' But you say, 'Whoever says to his father or mother, "Whatever profit you might have received from me is a gift to God"—then he need not honor his father or mother.' Thus you have made the commandment of God of no effect by your tradition. Hypocrites! Well did Isaiah prophesy about you, saying: 'These people draw near to Me with their mouth, and honor Me with their lips, but their heart is far from Me. And in vain they worship Me, teaching as doctrines the commandments*

of men.' When He had called the multitude to Himself, He said to them, "Hear and understand: Not what goes into the mouth defiles a man; but what comes out of the mouth, this defiles a man." Then His disciples came and said to Him, "Do You know that the Pharisees were offended when they heard this saying?" But He answered and said, "Every plant which My heavenly Father has not planted will be uprooted. Let them alone. They are blind leaders of the blind. And if the blind leads the blind, both will fall into a ditch." Then Peter answered and said to Him, "Explain this parable to us." So Jesus said, "Are you also still without understanding? Do you not yet understand that whatever enters the mouth goes into the stomach and is eliminated? But those things which proceed out of the mouth come from the heart, and they defile a man. For out of the heart proceed evil thoughts, murders, adulteries, fornications, thefts, false witness, blasphemies. These are the things which defile a man, but to eat with unwashed hands does not defile a man." Then Jesus went out from there and departed to the region of Tyre and Sidon. And behold, a woman of Canaan came from that region and cried out to Him, saying, "Have mercy on me, O Lord, Son of David! My daughter is severely demon-possessed." But He answered her not a word. And His disciples came and urged Him, saying, "Send her away, for she cries out after us." But He answered and said, "I was not sent except to the lost sheep of the house of Israel." Then she came and worshiped Him, saying, "Lord, help me!" But He answered and said, "It is not good to take the children's bread and throw it to the little dogs." And she said, "Yes, Lord, yet even the little dogs eat the crumbs which fall from their masters' table." Then Jesus answered and said to her, "O woman, great is your faith! Let it be to you as you desire." And her daughter was healed from that very hour (Matthew 15:1-28).

Here is an incident where both the Pharisees and a woman of Canaan had opportunities to be offended with the Lord. The contents of their heart confirmed what kingdom they served and determined their response to Jesus. First, the Pharisees were already offended with Jesus from the very start. They approached Jesus in order to question and trap Him. Jesus did not answer their question but rather questioned them. (When I am in a situation where I am being grilled by someone, I have learned to ask the Holy Spirit to show me the question He wants me to ask to answer the wrong motives of the other person. The Holy Spirit always gives me the question to ask them instead of answering their question. My dad, David Ward, also taught me how to do this.)

The Pharisees were asking Jesus why He transgressed the traditions of the elders. Notice that it was a tradition of man that Jesus was transgressing. However, Jesus responded to their question with a question: "Why do you transgress the commandment of God because of your tradition?" Jesus was telling the Pharisees that their traditions usurped the commandments of God. He educated the Pharisees on how their traditions made null the commandment of God, and He called them hypocrites.

Remember that this debate between the Pharisees and Jesus was public, so Jesus was publicly calling the Pharisees hypocrites. Moreover, Jesus called a multitude of people to Him and informed them that what comes out of a man's mouth defiles him. Jesus went into detail, stating that what comes out of the mouth flows from the heart.

> *For out of the heart proceed evil thoughts, murders, adulteries, fornications, thefts, false witness, blasphemies. These are the things which defile a man, but to eat with unwashed hands does not defile a man* (Matthew 15:19-20).

OFFENSE IS A SHOVEL

Jesus' disciples came to Him after this incident and told Him: Do You know that the Pharisees were offended when they heard this saying? (Matthew 15:12)

Notice that Jesus does not say, "Oh, I might need to go apologize to them, because I don't want them to be offended with Me."

Every plant which My heavenly Father has not planted will be uprooted. Let them alone. They are blind leaders of the blind. And if the blind leads the blind, both will fall into a ditch (Matthew 15:13-14).

This is the key revelation of the purpose of offense. The purpose of offense is to uproot whatever is not of God. It is a shovel. Let's read further to see a person who passes the offense test.

Right after Jesus' response, there is a Canaanite woman who has a demon-possessed daughter and is in need of a miracle. She did not come to Jesus with a formal delivery, looking dignified like the Pharisees. This Canaanite woman came to Jesus with a loud demonstration of desperation, screaming, *"Have mercy on me, O Lord, Son of David! My daughter is severely demon-possessed* (Matt. 15:22)." She made such a spectacle of herself in her desperation that the disciples wanted Jesus to send her away for crying out after the Lord.

The Lord at first did not respond to the Canaanite woman. This did not deter her from crying out after Him, though. When Jesus finally responded to the woman, He said that He was sent to the house of Israel. This did not deter the woman either; she started worshiping Jesus at that moment and cried out, "Lord, help me!" Next, Jesus explained to her that it was not good to give the children's bread to the dogs.

After being called a "dog," the woman responded to Jesus, *"Yes, Lord, yet even the little dogs eat the crumbs which fall from their masters' table* (Matt. 15:27)." She was still not offended by being called a dog and continued to call Jesus her Lord, saying that the dogs eat the crumbs that fall from their "master's table." The Canaanite woman was calling Jesus her master. Immediately, Jesus responded to the woman with, *"O woman, great is your faith! Let it be to you as you desire* (Matt. 15:22)." Her daughter was healed that hour.

SHOVEL IT OUT LORD!

When the Lord showed me this Scripture and the revelation of the purpose of offense, He had me focus on Jesus' response to the disciples when they said that the Pharisees were offended. Jesus responded that every plant not planted by His Father would be uprooted. In essence, Jesus was saying that anything not of the Kingdom of God would be uprooted. God uses offense to expose those ungodly things that are not of His Kingdom, as Jesus did here in the Scriptures.

If something planted is not of God's Kingdom, offense will shovel it out and uproot the very thing that is ungodly. When I am weeding in my garden, I use my hands to pull a lot of the weeds out of my garden. However, if a weed springs up I want to make sure that I get it by the root. It does not belong in my garden because it is a weed, not a flower or plant. I go to the back of my house, grab my shovel, and carry the shovel to the front yard. I put it to the ground, step my foot on the shovel, and go underneath the dirt where the weed's root is. I make sure that I literally get to the root of the problem so that it will not grow back in my garden.

Offense is a shovel to dig everything that is not of the Kingdom of God out of us, our family, our church, our community, and our nation. What does this look like? We have one of two responses when confronted with circumstances that offend us. We might feel righteous anger when someone has offended our Lord and Savior, or we might feel ungodly things in our hearts. God allows some offenses in order to uproot the ungodly things planted in our hearts.

This is why Jesus, after offending the Pharisees, called the people together and told them that the things that come out of the mouth defile a man. He told the disciples the meaning of defilement by stating:

> But those things which proceed out of the mouth come from the heart, and they defile a man. For out of the heart proceed evil thoughts, murders, adulteries, fornications, thefts, false witness, blasphemies. These are the things which defile a man, but to eat with unwashed hands does not defile a man (Matthew 15:18-20).

The evil in our hearts is uprooted by the offense that comes against us. Evil thoughts include everything that is ungodly. "Murders," mentioned here, refers to murdering people with words as well as physically. Jesus brought a higher standard when He came to fulfill the law on our behalf and be a sacrifice for us to enter eternal life with God. That standard was "grace." Jesus taught that murder was not the actual, physical killing of a person, but anyone could commit murder by being angry with their Christian brother or sister.

> You have heard that it was said to the people long ago, "Do not murder, and anyone who murders will be subject to judgment." But I tell you that anyone who is angry with his brother will be subject to judgment. Again, anyone who says to his brother, "Raca" is answerable to the Sanhedrin. But anyone who says, "You fool!" will be in danger of the fire of hell (Matthew 5:21-22 NIV).

The list of evils in the heart goes on to include adultery, fornication, thefts, false witness, and blasphemies. The standard for each of these evils is higher because of grace. Adultery is not just the actual act but even having the lust in your heart for another. False witness is telling untrue things about another person. All of these evils were exposed by Jesus when He offended the Pharisees and explained the defilement of the heart to His disciples. Offense will expose every ungodly thing that is planted in our hearts and defiling us.

The Pharisees did not repent for their error, even after being called hypocrites and having their human traditions exposed by the Word of God. They continued to be offended with Jesus. On the other hand, the Canaanite woman, who had been shushed by the disciples and called a dog by Jesus, did not become offended. Instead, she cried all the more for the healing of her daughter. Because she was not offended with Jesus and pressed in for her miracle, she received the very blessing from Jesus that she desired.

This is the greatest demonstration of the purpose of offense. Offense is a shovel. I love the Scripture in Jeremiah where God addresses the prophet, telling him that he is called to the nations.

> The word of the Lord came to me, saying, "Before I formed you in the womb I knew you, before you were born I set you apart; I appointed you as a prophet to the nations." "Ah, Sovereign Lord," I said, "I do not know how to speak; I am only a child." But the Lord said to me, "Do not say, 'I am

*only a child.' You must go to everyone I send you to and say whatever I command you. Do not be afraid of them, for I am with you and will rescue you," declares the Lord. Then the Lord reached out his hand and touched my mouth and said to me, "Now, I have put My words in your mouth. See, today I appoint you over nations and kingdoms to **uproot** and tear down, to destroy and overthrow, to build and to plant"* (Jeremiah 1:4-10 NIV).

Here too, God was calling Jeremiah the prophet to uproot. Jeremiah was one of the most offensive prophets in his day. He offended nearly everyone. In Jeremiah 18, the prophet gives the word of the Lord to God's people, and their response to him is one of offense.

They said, "Come, let's make plans against Jeremiah; for the teaching of the law by the priest will not be lost, nor will counsel from the wise, nor the word from the prophets. So come, let's attack him with our tongues and pay no attention to anything he says" (Jeremiah 18:18 NIV).

The people were so offended with Jeremiah that they banded together to scorn him publicly with their words (tongues) and ignored everything he said.

UPROOTING

When offense comes it is to expose the ungodly things in us, and if we yield ourselves to God's hand He will uproot it out of us by His Holy Spirit. I have been doing this for years since I had the revelation. The revelation came when my husband, Rich, and I went to a Spanish service. The pastor that was doing the Bible study taught on the Matthew 15 Scripture. He did not use it regarding offense but on being able to stand no matter what. The Spanish pastor used the Matthew 15 Scripture of the Pharisees and the Canaanite woman to instruct his congregation to stand in the midst of all adversity.

However, while listening to the Spanish teaching, the translation, and the pastor's demonstration or role-play of the Scripture, the revelation of offense sunk deep into my spirit. Offense is a shovel! Hallelujah! What a relief to know the purpose behind offense! To understand my reaction, you must know that I have a logical mind that sets out maps regarding everything that there is. When I was in law school, at the beginning of every class I knew that I had to understand the material to have the subject matter mapped in my brain. Then, when I took exams, I would be able to use my map of the material to answer the questions.

Now I had received a mapping for offense, and I was delighted. The Lord showed me that in our hearts, because we are born into a fallen world, many things are planted in us that are not of God. God wants to uproot those ungodly things in our hearts by His Holy Spirit. Sometimes, the uprooting is done through conviction of our sins, and we repent. However, sometimes God uses offense to uproot things that are implanted in our hearts. He told me that anytime I am feeling offended with someone, my first reaction should be to ask the Holy Spirit to expose anything in me that is contrary to God.

For example, the other day I was on my way back from a women's conference with a bunch of my sisters in Christ. We had been to a four-day conference and had spent a lot of time with each other. To say the least, when you spend a lot of time with others, things can come out of a person that might not be lovely. During this time, I was on the cusp of receiving a great deliverance from the stronghold of a controlling spirit that had operated against me most of my life, and it happened to be at the same time as the conference.

As we were getting ready to return home, the driver of the car wanted to put something right beside my arm and leg that would restrict my comfort in the vehicle. We were in a huge SUV that had several seats in it, and I happened to be in the back one with my seat nearly half the size of everyone else's. I had sat there the entire four days without complaint. Moreover, the luggage in the back kept sliding on me every time we went over a bump or turned. My ability to tolerate any more discomfort was fragile, and I was still overcoming the issue with the controlling spirit. When my sister went to put the item by me, I was more than a bit bothered. As I was helping her get the item packed in the back where I had been the past four days, she abruptly told me to be careful with her item.

After her words, I became very bothered and angry. She had overlooked me as a person. There was no physical way I could move an inch with the item beside me, while everyone else had the comfort of huge seats. I was already trying to keep things from falling on my head and against my body every time the luggage moved. I was offended.

When I got out of the car to leave with my husband, I did not hug my sister. I had to be swayed by her to give her a hug. Truthfully, I did not want to hug her. It took me a couple of days to deal with this offense. I had to dig deep with the Lord and ask Him to expose what was not of God inside my heart. Many times before, it only took me a few minutes to get to this point and ask the Holy Spirit to expose what was not of God in me. However, this time it took much longer. I did not want the offense; I detested the offense and still had to seek the Lord regarding what ungodly thing was in my heart.

Finally, God showed me that this was the culmination of my struggle with control. I had often been controlled and was always expected to be a slave, and I had not had the love of Christ in me. I looked at what God was telling me. My divine deliverance from the control issues was not the same as my need for the love of Christ. Although this sister might have been trying to be a little controlling—making sure her item was going to be taken care of regardless of my expense—I was to show her unconditional love. I failed this test of love because I was offended. I know that I will get this test again, though, and I hope to pass the next one.

On other occasions, when my husband and I are in "discussions," there are times when I can be offended. During those times, I remind myself that I am to love and honor my husband no matter what the cost, and I refuse to be offended. That is my ultimate goal, and I do this many times. However, there are times when, in my weakness, I do get offended, and I go to my husband and repent later. In every instance, though, the Holy Spirit is showing me what is not of God in me.

SISTER, SISTER!

When we are in relationship with our sisters we do not need to be offended with one another. Sisters love each other and are in unity as Psalms states.

> *How good and pleasant it is when brothers live together in unity! It is like precious oil poured on the head, running down on the beard, running down on Aaron's beard, down upon the collar of his robes. It is as if the dew of Hermon were falling on Mount Zion. For there the Lord bestows His blessing, even life forevermore* (Psalm 133 NIV).

Offense is the biggest hindrance to unity in relationships. There is power in unity. The enemy hates this, so he tries to sow discord or disunity between people of the faith through offense.

Sisters in the Lord are to seek God when we get offended with one another. We are to ask Him to expose contrary things in *our* hearts and not the other sister's heart. We cannot change people; only the Holy Spirit of God can change others. Our job is to seek God about changing ourselves in order to become more in the image of Christ.

Many times when I am in a circumstance with another sister in which I might feel offended, my first response is to ask God to expose what ungodly thing is in my heart by His Holy Spirit. *Every time* I ask God to do this He is faithful. Sometimes He shows me that it is pride that is in my heart; I ask Him to remove it from me, and immediately afterward I have great peace. Other times it might be jealousy, ambition, selfishness, or something else. We must understand that offense comes to shovel things out of us that are ungodly.

By contrast, if another sister is offended by you, you should help her overcome the offense if you can. For example, the other day my husband and youngest son and I were sitting at a red light, and another woman and her daughter were in front of us waiting for the signal to turn green. The signal turned green, and we only had a short amount of time before the light turned red. The woman and her daughter in front of us were looking off to the right, unaware that the light was green. After a few seconds, I tapped my horn one time to let them know the light was green. From their expression, you would have thought that I had laid on my horn impatiently, which was certainly not the case. However, the enemy took the opportunity to magnify the one tap of my horn and their ignorance of the light turning green to create an offense in both the mother and daughter.

As soon as we pulled up to the store and got out of our cars, I explained to the woman that the light had been green for some time and I had noticed she and her daughter were looking elsewhere. I told her that my one tap on the horn was just to alert them that the light was green, not to be impatient and force them to move. She and I later ended up having a pleasant conversation about her blue jeans. I could have simply ignored her offense with me or expected her to "take it to the Lord." However, as her sister in Christ, I knew that God wanted me to walk her through the offense and help her see that the enemy had laid a trap for her to be offended needlessly. Afterward, I felt that the circumstance gave me an opportunity to have a new friend.

In dealing with my family and friends, I do the same thing when there is an offense due to miscommunication, misunderstanding, et cetera. The enemy enjoys sowing offense between people through whatever means he can. Therefore, we have to become peacemakers on the earth to help people get over offenses whenever the Holy Spirit shows us. A favorite Scripture of mine is, *"Blessed are the peacemakers, for they will be called sons of God"* (Matt. 5:9 NIV). We become peacemakers when we help others get over offenses either from us or from elsewhere.

HELP ME, GOD, TO BE WITHOUT OFFENSE

Ask God to send His Holy Spirit each time you are offended to expose ungodly things that are planted in your heart. A word of caution here—the Lord has shown me that, when offense comes, if we do not yield to the uprooting of ungodly things in our hearts then we will be uprooted. How will we be uprooted? We might leave a church, a job, a marriage, or a godly relationship. If we do not allow the offense to shovel things out of our hearts, then the root of offense will eventually uproot us.

Also, the Lord has shown me that freedom from offense is for the person who has been offended, not the offender. The offender many times does not realize that they have offended a person. The sister from the women's conference did not realize she offended me. I carried that offense, and I needed to get rid of it.

It truly is possible to live a life free from ungodly offense. I know this because I have walked in seasons when I totally yielded myself to God and sought to stay low and humble in Him. I did not seek my own glory or my own will, but rather delighted in what pleased my Father. Knowing that offense toward others did not please Him, I delighted in seeing how unoffended I could be with others, especially when there were plenty of opportunities for offense.

The apostle Paul shows us that it is possible to live a life free of offense.

> *And this I pray, that your love may abound still more and more in knowledge and all discernment, that you may approve the things that are excellent, that you may be sincere and without offense till the day of Christ, being filled with the fruits of righteousness which are by Jesus Christ, to the glory and praise of God* (Philippians 1:9-11).

Paul the apostle prays that our love will abound more and more in knowledge and discernment. This knowledge and discernment helps us approve things that are excellent and keeps us sincere and without offense until the day of Christ. That means until Christ returns! Hallelujah, it is possible to be without offense all the days of our lives. I love using contemplative prayer each morning with the Lord (praying the Word to God with contemplation). I can tell you that when you use this passage in prayer to the Lord, the Holy Spirit releases a peace that is beyond our understanding, and it is as if the peace of God rules in your heart.

Unoffended

QUESTIONS:

1. Are there any specific areas in your life where you have been offended with those you have relationships with? Identify those areas.

2. Do you watch shows are read magazines that glorify offense? If so, stop allowing those materials in your "eye gate" and "ear gate."

3. Can you give all of these areas over to God and ask His Holy Spirit to expose the ungodly things planted in your heart?

REPENTANCE FOR SECTION III SINS

In closing, here is a prayer to pray in order to repent from any of the sins listed throughout Section III. We need to pause a moment and look at all the sins throughout this section, and after allowing God to search our hearts, we can pray. Look at all the questions throughout Section III and read your answers to them. After a couple of months, go back through the list and answer the questions again. If you have prayed for repentance, then your answers will change within a week and assuredly within two months.

PRAYER

Father God, I invite You now to pull out of me anything that is vile and not of You. I ask Your Holy Spirit to search my heart and bring to mind anything that I have been doing that is in disobedience to Your Word. Forgive me if I have been judgmental, prideful, gossiping, covetous, or offensive toward anyone. I thank You for this revelation of how I am to act to other sisters in Christ and what I need to be mindful of in keeping clean hands and a pure heart before You. Thank You Jesus for the blood You shed which covers all my sins. Thank You for making me a new creature and setting my foot on the narrow path.

*Accepted
In Christ*

SECTION FOUR

Many times in my life I have looked for acceptance by others. I always felt as though I was unacceptable. What I discovered was the very reason I felt that way was because the only place I could find total acceptance was in Christ.

> *Blessed be the God and Father of our Lord Jesus Christ, who has blessed us with every spiritual blessing in the heavenly places in Christ, just as **He chose us in Him before the foundation of the world**, that we should be holy and without blame before*

Him in love, **having predestined us to adoption as sons by Jesus Christ to Himself,** *according to the good pleasure of His will, to the praise of the glory of His grace, by which* **He made us accepted in the Beloved** (Ephesians 1:3-6).

chapter

11

The Four-Year-Old Artist

Webster's Dictionary defines "accept" as "to take; receive; to receive favorably; approve; to understand as having certain meaning; to believe."[1] When we desire to be accepted, we are not asking merely for others to "accept" us, as in the moment. We want them to accept *all* of us. That includes our successes, mistakes, and dreams. This compilation makes up a person. I have heard an analogy of a little girl coloring a picture and have modified it for women in Christ; I desire for women to see themselves.

COLORING FOR GOD

Imagine yourself as a little four-year-old girl coloring a picture for your father. Although coloring a house and trees, you are really coloring yourself on the paper. Then you take it to your father, and as most four-year-olds so proudly do, you hold it behind your back while you walk in the room expectantly to show him your work of art. You turn to your father and say, "Daddy, I've got something to show you," at which he turns to look at you and wait for your presentation. With great pleasure, you pull from behind you the picture and hold it up to him asking, "How do you like it, Daddy?"

You wait anxiously for the response, expecting an affirmation of how incredible your work is and that it is the best piece of work that he has ever seen. What you receive is a great big, "Oh my!" He smiles from ear to ear with great joy and stands up to pick you up while you hold the art work in your hands. He delights in the work that you have done. He looks at the little details you have meticulously managed to do on your own. He is caught up in the great choice of color you have picked out and describes the great emotions it brings out of his heart. "How could you have ever done this? You are my little Picasso," he says. "I love your work and I believe it is the best that I've ever seen." He places you on his lap while he sits down and smiles at you, looks into your eyes, and says, "It's beautiful, just like you."

Do You Like My Picture?

What is really happening when we, as the four-year-old, show our father the picture and ask his opinion? We are getting an opinion, not of how our father likes our picture, but instead of how he likes us. That is what we do with our life. Our life is a "picture," so to speak, and as we walk throughout our life with our joys, traumas, mistakes, and sadnesses we are asking others the question, "How do you like who I am in the midst of my life?" The response we are seeking is not how others like the way we are living our lives, but how they like us and whether or not they accept us.

Ugly Pictures

Imagine yourself at your current age feeling that, due to your bad behaviors and choices, others are pushing you away. It is no different if you are the four-year-old girl who is coloring a picture, and although it may be ugly and unbecoming, you are still holding it up and asking, "How do you like my picture?" Most of the time we get a response from people that it is "ugly" and that they do not like it. In essence, they are not saying that they don't like the picture, but that they do not like us.

When I was struggling with alcohol in the sorority, although my sisters were unhappy with my problems and my bad choices, I felt that they were unhappy with *me*—the person God had created. That person was still there, in bondage to so much—pleasing man, feeling rejected, and in fear of man. When they agreed to dismiss me from the sorority and the fraternity, it affirmed my belief that they did not accept me. I could not separate my sins from who I was. The result of people telling me they hated my "picture"—my life—was that I felt unaccepted, unlovable, and unvalued.

However, God the Father made us accepted. That means that when the Creator, God, created man and woman, He put in them all the ingredients that make them up. One of the ingredients was *acceptance*. He made us to be *accepted*. If we are accepted, what doesn't exist in us? Rejection does not live in us because it is contrary to acceptance. We may have "messed up" in life, making many mistakes and committing sins that are so horrendous to us, but it does not mean that we are no longer accepted. It only means that at that time, we were coloring an unlovely picture; it does not make us unacceptable to the Father.

An Angry Heart

I felt that I was unworthy to come back to God after I had been so wrapped up in sin. I had a drinking problem which led to unhealthy relationships and caused much anger. I had so much bitterness and resentment in the core of my heart that many people did not want to be around me. It was a miracle that I was still alive, because there had been so many times as a single mom when I became overwhelmed and wanted to "end it." Life was more than I could handle in my own strength, and I felt as though I was unable to do anything at the time for my two boys.

I did love my sons, took them to church, and functioned enough to get through the day, but deep down I was depressed, overwhelmed, and thought that I could not withstand one more thing. I was in serious trouble. Everyone knew it—my family, friends, my children's teachers, my college professors, and my neighbors. I was experiencing failure and rejection again, and at the same time, I was being judged. Some people asked me, "Why don't you get yourself together and act right?" If I could have at the time, I would have. On the other hand, I was in bondage, feeling rejected, being despised, and feeling like a "bad girl" who was unable to get herself together. I did not understand that the Father was the only One who could get me out of my pain and sin.

THEY HATE MY PICTURE!

As that four-year-old girl I was holding up my picture that I had colored to the world. Everyone around me was saying, "I hate your picture; your picture is ugly." What I heard from the world was, "I despise you and you are a pitiful excuse for a person." I was coming to the end of myself, feeling hopeless.

I grieved over my circumstances in life and who I had become in the midst of them. It had gotten to the point that I began hearing voices, which really scared me because I had worked in outpatient psychiatry as a social worker with people who heard voices. I was suicidal and had planned in my head the exact location on the interstate in Birmingham, Alabama, where I would end my life by running off of the bridge by the exit ramp. Turning to God became my only option. I wanted so desperately to be loved.

Artist Colorings

QUESTIONS:

1. From the Section I, Chapter 1 questions, look at your story and pick out areas in which you might have felt as though you were not being accepted. What are the specific times you felt unaccepted by others? What were the times that you were acting ungodly and others did not accept you?

2. Can you give all of your pictures to Jesus? Can you give Him all of you and allow Him to cleanse you of all of your sin?

3. What has kept you from giving all of yourself to Jesus? What is holding you back? What do you need to confront that is keeping you from total surrender to Jesus?

ENDNOTE

1. *Webster's New World Dictionary of the American Language* 2nd College Edition (New York: Prentice Hall Press, 1986).

12

Made Accepted

God made us to be accepted in Him, not in man. The only place we can truly find unconditional acceptance of all that we are is in God. He accepts us right where we are and doesn't require that we be "all together" so that He might work with us. On the contrary, He wants us broken before Him and emptied of ourselves. It is necessary to reach this point so that in Him we will find who we truly are. It's as though we are returning to a loving Father to whom we take all of our pictures, both ugly and pretty ones, and no matter what we show Him, He will tell us He loves us.

CREATED IN HIS IMAGE

Who else better to love us than He that created us? God is love.

> *And we know (understand, recognize, are conscious of, by observation and by experience) and believe (adhere to and put faith in and rely on) the love God cherishes for us.* **God**

is love, and he who dwells and continues in love dwells and continues in God, and God dwells and continues in him (1 John 4:16 AMP).

We desire to be loved because that is what God is, and in so being, He created us in the image of the Trinity—Himself, the Son, and the Holy Spirit. In the beginning, God said, *"Let Us make man in Our image according to Our likeness..."* (Gen. 1:26). Therefore, if He is love and He made us in His image, then the Word says we are love.

In the act of giving and receiving, in order to get love we have to receive it. Webster's defines "receive" as "to encounter; experience; to apprehend mentally." In order for us to truly feel accepted in love we have to encounter and experience the Father's love. It is done by mentally apprehending the Father's love for us. For example, for many of us, while we were growing up we naturally understood that our parents or guardians loved us. (I realize that this is not the case for everyone, but only imagine with me.)

DROWNING

When I was six years old I thought that I could swim well. I went to the diving board, jumped off, and before I knew it, I sank to the bottom of the pool instead of floating to the top. I realized then that I could not swim. My mom was fully dressed in her pants and top and still had her shoes on. She was afraid for my safety and jumped in with everything still on in order to rescue me. I *experienced* her love for me because of her *act* of coming to my rescue. Likewise, we have to *experience* the Father's love for us by looking at His act of love toward us. His acts of love are demonstrated when we reflect back over our lives and can see moments where we were protected, felt special, or saw extraordinary things occur. These acts confirm His love toward us.

As I look back over my life now, I see so many times during my drinking and partying life in my early twenties when I put myself into positions in which I really should have been taken advantage of by a guy. I could have died or any number of horrible happenings. I realize that it was by the grace of God and His infinite mercy that I am even alive. I can see the times when God has kept me when I should have fallen. For example, when I was a single mom living in the house my ex-husband and I had shared, I should not have been able to remain in the house after he left. However, God made a way and provided. My ex-husband and I were only in the house together for 3 years. Since he left, it has been my home for over 11 years, 4 years spent as a single mom. God is so good. I saw God's love for me. It was at that time that I experienced His love because I mentally apprehended it.

How Has God Loved You?

Have you survived an illness, an addiction, an abuser, or some traumatic circumstances? Have you seen times in your life when extraordinary things have happened to you? For example, has someone said something before you wanted to kill yourself, has your favorite song come on the radio when you thought that you couldn't take it anymore, and so on? Don't think for one minute that everything is happenstance! God is the Creator, Choreographer, and Keeper of your life. Open yourself up to seeing it and giving yourself to Him so that He might fully give you everything that He desires for you to have.

> For **I know the thoughts and plans that I have for you,** says the Lord, thoughts and plans **for welfare and peace and not for evil,** to give you **hope in your final outcome.** Then you will call upon Me, and you will come and pray to Me, and I will hear and heed you. Then you will seek Me, inquire for, and require Me [as a vital necessity] and find Me when you search for Me with all your heart (Jeremiah 29:11-13 AMP).

This Scripture speaks volumes. I read this repeatedly while going through my struggles as a single mom. Initially, I could not understand God's love for me because I had experienced so much devastation and rejection. Although His love was imprinted over my life, I was wearing lenses that were tainted. Just as that breakup in my junior year of high school—although it was such a minor thing in life—was magnified because I was not able to see it clearly, I was still viewing life from the lenses of rejection and feeling unaccepted. In order to move to a feeling of acceptance, we have to put on new lenses. Being loved is an action on our part. We choose to take off the tainted lenses of the enemy's lies that say we are not valuable and insignificant, and we put on the lenses of God.

INSEPARABLE LOVE

Paul states:

> *For I am persuaded beyond doubt (am sure) that neither death nor life, nor angels nor principalities, nor things impending and threatening nor things to come, nor powers, nor height nor depth, nor anything else in all creation will be able to separate us from the love of God which is in Christ Jesus our Lord* (Romans 8:38-39 AMP).

Almighty God will not allow *anything* to separate us from His love. He covers anything and everything possible that could separate us from His love, and it is clear that *nothing* will. God is love, and therefore everything that He does is motivated from that position of what He *is*. He sent His only Son to die on the Cross for our sins, and if you were the only person on the earth, He would still have sent His Son because it is His desire that none should perish.

> *For God so greatly loved and dearly prized the world that He [even] gave up His only begotten (unique) Son, so that whoever believes in (trusts in, clings to, relies on) Him shall not perish (come to destruction, be lost) but have eternal (everlasting) life* (John 3:16 AMP).

Why would the Creator of the universe want to create us only to have us out of His reach? Do we as loving parents have children so that we can give them away or torture them? Of course not! Would we not give our very lives for our children? As the Bibles states:

> *If you then, evil as you are, know how to give good and advantageous gifts to your children, how much more will*

*your Father Who is in Heaven [perfect as He is] give good
and advantageous things to those who keep on asking Him!*
(Matthew 7:11 AMP)

It is arrogant for us to believe God would not love us while we as mere
human beings have more love for people than God does. One might think
this is a strong statement. However, the enemy is out to deceive us, and if
we can truly see what he is doing then we will be on guard. Satan "fell" from
Heaven because of his pride (see Isaiah 14:12-16). Most of the time, my "poor
me" insecurities are really offensive to God because they are saying to God, "I
don't believe You over satan."

BATTLING THE LIE

When the enemy comes and tells us that God will not love us because we
are "unholy" and have done so many horrible things, we are to tell him that
he is a liar. We are to cast down the lie, as is stated by Paul, and take *every*
thought captive.

> *We demolish arguments and every pretension that sets itself up
> against the knowledge of God, and we take captive every thought
> to make it obedient to Christ* (2 Corinthians 10:5 NIV).

We take a thought captive by "measuring" it whenever it enters our mind.
We measure a thought by judging it against the Word at the point of entry. If
it does not line up with the Word, it is not from God. How do we know if it's
a thought from the enemy? Paul states in Philippians:

> *Finally, brothers, **whatever is true, whatever is noble, whatever
> is right, whatever is pure, whatever is lovely, whatever is
> admirable**—if anything is excellent or praiseworthy—think
> about such things* (Philippians 4:8 NIV).

The things that are scripturally true, noble, right, pure, lovely, admirable,
excellent, and praiseworthy are from God. If it does not fall into one of those
categories, it is not from God.

There is no gray area; it is black and white. Therefore, if a thought comes up that is contrary to that list, what we need to do then is use Scripture to throw it out. Some awesome Scriptures to use are Second Corinthians 10:5, John 3:16, Jeremiah 29:11-13, First John 4:16, Romans 8:38-39, and First Corinthians 2:16.

Made Accepted

QUESTIONS:

1a. Do you feel accepted by Christ? If you do, describe how you feel accepted. If not, describe why you think Christ would not accept you and go to Question B.

1b. Do you believe that Christ came to die for your sins and reunite you with Father God? If so, then use the Scriptures in this chapter to confront disbelief until you believe that you are accepted and then date it when you come into that truth. If not, then seek a trusted mentor in order to work through this lie.

2. Are there times in your own life in which you felt God's love? Look over your story again in Section I, Chapter 1, and identify times throughout your story where you specifically felt God's love. If you have trouble with this, then you need to confess the Scriptures in this chapter again until you come into the truth and then answer this question.

3. Can you share with other women how God has made you accepted in Him? If not, then continue to confess the Scriptures until you have confidence in being accepted in Christ.

4. When do you feel as though you are not accepted? Is it a sin in which you are struggling or a behavior that is ungodly?

5. What Scriptures in this chapter do you need to confess to assure yourself when you experience times of being unaccepted?

c h a p t e r

13

Learning to Receive Love

I married Rich in December 2001, and for the first couple of years of our marriage I could not grasp the fact that he "loved me." I had been hurt so much from past broken relationships that I believed he would leave me. After my nine-month first marriage at 19 years old—a relationship of physical and mental torture—I was single for a couple of years. Then I married a young man right before he started medical school, and after he completed his residency program and we had been married eight years, he fell in love with another woman and left me as a single mom of one- and six-year-old boys. I was even more devastated after that breakup. To say the very least, my understanding of *love* and being *accepted* was distorted. After being a single mother for four years, this distortion bled into my relationship with my current husband.

"YOU ARE SO UNLOVABLE"

In my past relationships, I fought emotionally because of the rejection. I felt akin to how I did when I stood up to the bully at the bus stop as a teenager.

It was as though life had taken me over its head and thrown me down and knocked all of the wind out of me. I felt like life was saying, "You are so unlovable." Before I knew it, I was doing the only thing I knew—fighting. I would scream back at life, "I am too lovable! And no matter how many times you tell me I'm unlovable and knock me down, I'm going to get back up in your face, Life, and tell you how lovable I am!"

THE BOXING RING

I remember Rich saying to me on many occasions, "Robin, why don't you let me love you?" I was thinking to myself, "Duh, that is what I'm trying to do; I'm standing here, and I'm saying I want you to love me." For example, early in our relationship there would be many times that our disagreements would lead into an argument. After we made up, I still kept a wall up between Rich and I. Many times, he would in his own way try to love me but I simply would not let him. I had created rules under which he could approach me, according to my comfort zone. I had, in essence, set up an emotional boxing ring. "In this corner, weighing..."

However, over time the Holy Spirit showed me the damage inflicted by what I was doing. I was in an emotional boxing ring, and as Rich would approach me to love me, I would put up my "boxing gloves" and say, "All right; love me. Take a punch; prove you care." How can anyone approach someone like that? They cannot.

I had been so hurt over broken and failed relationships where I felt rejected and unloved that I went into my relationship with Rich as a boxing match, hoping that we would last several rounds. I believed that what had been done to me in the past was going to happen at any moment in our relationship. I couldn't "rest in his love;" I simply danced around the ring, and when I felt as though I could trust him I might let him get close putting up my gloves. On the other hand, when I felt threatened, looking through the lenses of rejection, I would put those two gloves up—the ones that said, "I knew he would not love me," and "I knew that I could not trust him." I would use them every time we got into a disagreement. I felt that when we disagreed he did not love me and I couldn't trust him to love me. Instead, what was going on was that we were becoming one flesh. When two become one, it is, to say the least, challenging.

I thank God for Rich, because I look back now and see how much I have changed and how he literally has had to be God's agent and love the hurt out of me. The church that I attend also experienced this when I first went there after my divorce as a single mother. Praise God that it is a loving church; that was exactly what I needed—love. Since my husband and church family did this, it literally helped to catapult me into healing.

REVELATION OF LOVE

I wanted so desperately to be loved. Finally, I received the revelation of what Rich had meant. I was so busy trying to get him to love me by doing works. When my works and actions displeased him and we got in disagreements, I felt as though he was not disagreeing with my acts but that he didn't love me. He wanted me to know by faith that he loved me, which was not anything that I could work for; he simply wanted to give me love.

We do this to the Father as well. We are so busy doing works to get Him to love us—not doing "that sin," going to church, being nice, and so on. We are trying to *convince* Him to love us. However, His love is received as an act of faith, not works. We need to be still and *let* Him love us. Webster's Dictionary defines "let" as "to allow or permit." When we let someone love us we give permission: "Yes. I will allow them to love me." We are allowing that person to love us.

It is the same with God. God already told us that He has made us accepted in Him and that He is love, and as a result He wants to love us. We, in turn, have to agree that He is love and give Him permission to love us or we will not experience it. Complete love is not unilateral; love is bilateral. This means that one can love another person, but love is truly experienced when the other person *receives* the love and turns around to give it back. Therefore, God loves us and we receive His love, and in turn we love God and He receives our love.

Seeing Jesus' Eyes

We can intellectualize Jesus' payment for our life, knowing that we in our own righteousness cannot get into an eternal Heaven. It is only by His righteousness (right standing) in God that we enter. I did intellectualize Jesus' payment for my sins for many years. I knew that God loved me and that Jesus died for me in my head—my intellect. However, I could not fully comprehend it until I *received* His love in my heart. When I really understood what Jesus had done to save me from eternal damnation, it was as though this huge door opened. Behind the door was this mind-blowing event that was indescribable, a depth and width that was beyond my understanding. I was still *seeing* it, but I couldn't totally comprehend it upon first glance.

I had been saved for a long time—ever since I was six years old. Almost 30 years later, I had not yet experienced Jesus the way I did when I came to a new understanding of His sacrifice. All of a sudden, *I saw.* My eyes were opened to see Jesus, not the act, to see His face, not the scene. I was able to focus on Jesus more than the circumstance in which I saw Him—on the Cross. Then, I saw how beautiful and loving He was. Jesus is love. I imagined His eyes and saw them in my mind. I looked at the furrow of His brow in my mind. It was about Jesus in the midst of the circumstances. What He did for us was out of His love. *"Greater love has no one than this, that he lay down his life for his friends"* (John 15:13 NIV). Jesus had come to earth to lay His life down so that I would be *accepted* into eternity with God through Him. I understood that I was truly accepted in Jesus.

Salvation

After knowing how much the Father loves us and understanding our acceptance in Christ, there is a question: Will we receive Him as the Lover of our soul and allow Him to come into our heart? How do we do that? We confess with our mouth what we feel in our heart.

Right now, if you want to receive Him as your Lord and Savior, confess that you believe in Him as Lord, and believe in your heart that God gave Him as a sacrifice and raised Him from the dead. The Scripture in Romans states salvation is received by this act.

> *That if you confess with your mouth, "Jesus is Lord," and believe in your heart that God raised Him from the dead, you will be saved. For it is with your heart that you believe and are justified, and it is with your mouth that you confess and are saved. As the Scripture says, "Anyone who trusts in Him will never be put to shame"* (Romans 10:9-11 NIV).

If you want to follow in obedience, walking in salvation with Jesus, all you have to do is pray a prayer. It is a simple prayer that goes like this:

> *Father, I believe that Jesus is Lord, and I know that He came to earth and died for my sins and that You raised Him from the dead. I want Jesus to come into my life as my Lord and Savior. I receive your love. Amen.*

There is no need to do any flips or quote ten Scriptures. It is simply believing, trusting, and receiving on your part. It is not a *ritual* but a *relationship*.

LOVING JESUS

As discussed earlier, to really experience love it has to be a bilateral relationship. How can we show our love to God? Our love to God is demonstrated when we keep His commandments.

> *Whoever has My commands and obeys them, he is the one who loves Me. He who loves Me will be loved by My Father, and I too will love him and show Myself to him* (John 14:21 NIV).

God has commandments listed throughout the Scriptures. Most people know the Ten Commandments. Jesus tells us in the Gospels how to love our neighbor, how to treat the gifts of God, how to look at ourselves, how to look at others, and so on. Therefore, we need to read the Bible to discover all the commandments He has written. In Hosea 4:6, the Word states that His people perish for lack of knowledge.

Many Christians are experiencing attacks from the enemy because they don't read the Word. The enemy has a foothold because they do not have the knowledge from the Word that they need in order to set them free. It's similar to having a parachute, jumping out of the plane, and not knowing how to open it up. If a person does not open up the Word they are not going to know how to use it.

Receiving Love

QUESTIONS:

1. Are you saved? If so, then great! If not, do you want salvation? If you do want salvation, then *pray the prayer above* for salvation and receive Jesus as your Lord and Savior and date it here.

2. Do you have a problem trusting God? If you do, look over your story in Section I, Chapter 1, and identify times you did not trust God. Why did you not take your hurt to Him? How did you feel let down?

3. If you felt let down by God or you could not trust Him, repent for unbelief and ask God to forgive you. Then ask His Holy Spirit to lead you into all truth through His Word. Write down the Scriptures you can confess from the Section IV chapters that will help you come into truth.

4. Are you loving Jesus? Are you obedient to the Word? If so, what are you doing to show it? If not, then what do you need to change in order to show Jesus your love for Him?

5. Is your distrust of God or your problem receiving love from God affecting other areas of your life (personal, career, social, etc.)? If so, then what Scripture can you confess in order to get the truth into you?

14

Kissing His Feet

To be in Christ means we have to understand that our genetic makeup includes acceptance. In addition, we have to take off the lenses of rejection and put on the lenses of truth by casting down the lie that we are not accepted. Understand that while we were sinners—not perfect—Christ died for us (see Rom. 5:8). Therefore, we can come to Him as we are, like that four-year-old girl, show Him our picture (our life), and trust that He will accept us right where we are, as we are. Learn how to receive His love by reflecting on times that He has demonstrated His love. In reading the Bible, we learn who Jesus really is—the Lover of our souls. We demonstrate our love toward Him by keeping His commandments and being obedient.

THE WOMAN THAT JESUS TOUCHED

Let's look at the woman who washed Jesus' feet.

Now one of the Pharisees invited Jesus to have dinner with him, so He went to the Pharisee's house and reclined at the table. When a woman who had lived a sinful life in that town learned that Jesus was eating at the Pharisee's house, she brought an alabaster jar of perfume, and as she stood behind Him at His feet weeping, she began to wet His feet with her tears. Then she wiped them with her hair, kissed them and poured perfume on them. When the Pharisee who had invited Him saw this, he said to himself, "If this man were a prophet, he would know who is touching Him and what kind of woman she is—that she is a sinner." Jesus answered him, "Simon, I have something to tell you." "Tell me, Teacher," he said. "Two men owed money to a certain moneylender. One owed him five hundred denarii, and the other fifty. Neither of them had the money to pay him back, so he canceled the debts of both. Now which of them will love him more?" Simon replied, "I suppose the one who had the bigger debt canceled." "You have judged correctly," Jesus said. Then He turned toward the woman and said to Simon, "Do you see this woman? I came into your house. You did not give Me any water for My feet, but she wet My feet with her tears and wiped them with her hair. You did not give Me a kiss, but this woman, from the time I entered, has not stopped kissing My feet. You did not put oil on My head, but she has poured perfume on My feet. **Therefore, I tell you, her many sins have been forgiven—for she loved much. But he who has been forgiven little loves little.*** *Then Jesus said to her, "Your sins are forgiven." The other guests began to say among themselves, "Who is this who even forgives sins?" Jesus said to the woman, "Your faith has saved you; go in peace"* (Luke 7:36-50 NIV).

KEEPING MY SIN

I was in bondage to alcohol, promiscuous, angry, and full of sin when I came back to Jesus. I felt so filthy, so used by the world, and so unlovely.

Before this, I had still had sin in my life, but I had not brought it all to Jesus in order that I might be forgiven. I still wanted my sin and Jesus, too. Therefore, my sin had been forgiven little because I didn't give it all to Him. As a result, I loved little—as is seen in the Scripture—because I was not surrendering all of me. I was caught up in myself, clueless to the world around me.

Eventually, my sin added up and it became more painful to live with. I came to a point where I had never felt so unloved in my life, and it was unbearable. Then one day, after I sought Him with all that was in me and placed *all* of my sins in front of Him, I felt Jesus' love for me. Like the woman in this story, I placed all of my ugliness before a loving Savior and showed Him all the horrible things that might cause Him to turn away or refuse me.

WILL HE REFUSE ME?

The thing that had turned everyone else in the world away from me was the very thing that the Savior took from me. He did not say, "Only bring your purity to Me and the rest has to be left behind." On the contrary, Jesus wanted me to bring my sin *to Him*—my ugly pictures. He accepted me in the midst of my ugly pictures. He wanted my sin in order to cleanse me of it. He died on a Cross for my sin, and only Jesus is able to take my ugly, gross sins and wash me of them—to cleanse me.

After truly surrendering all of myself to Jesus, I saw Him in my mind. It was so clear—a secret place where I have my Jesus. It's a place where I can go to and feel unconditional love—a love that is so indescribable. All I can do is weep when I come to that place. I'm literally melting inside with the love of Jesus. I usually come to this place when I worship the Lord. When I come, I can imagine how the woman who anointed the feet of our Savior felt. She felt the love of Jesus and became undone. There was no way she could show her appreciation, say thank you, or even demonstrate her gratefulness. All she knew to do was to show her "undoneness" to Jesus. She had been forgiven so much, and because of the forgiveness she *loved* much. God is love.

LOOKING WEIRD TO THE WORLD

When we come to the place of total surrender and put on *much love*, we then look strange to the world. This woman had disclosed something that was so out of the ordinary that even those around her rebuked her. However, she did it anyway, without regard for their opinions of her. When we get to the point of fullness of love in Christ, we lose thought of what others might say about us.

First, the woman Jesus touched wept over His feet. When I returned to the Lord, I wept many tears over my sins, because I had done many wrong things and had not understood it before. I used to think sin was my desire to do something that "felt good." However, upon returning to the Lord, what I saw was my first love—Jesus—who felt as though I had left Him for another lover. Upon the discovery, I was cut to the core of my heart. Oh my! He loves me so much! I looked at how much I had hurt Jesus, not made Him mad. That is why satan wants to paint a picture of a big Father in Heaven with a paddle and a stern rebuke on His face. However, that is not who God is when His beautiful daughters are away from Him. The Father is longing for their return.

WETTING HIS FEET

After wetting the feet of Jesus with her tears, the woman poured her finest possession of ointment on His feet. She poured a fragrance on His feet. Everything that had been a stench to all those around her had now been turned into a sweet fragrance. Likewise, after surrendering all of my sin and giving it over to Jesus, He made my life of stench and grossness to now smell of a sweet fragrance.

We overcome by the blood of the Lamb and the word of our testimony (see Rev. 12:11). My life was turned into a sweet fragrance. That which appeared to be a horrible stench actually was made fragrant after I left everything at the feet of my Savior. Paul writes:

> But thanks be to God, who **always leads us in triumphal procession** in Christ and through us **spreads everywhere the**

*fragrance of the knowledge of Him. For **we are to God the aroma of Christ** among those who are being saved and those who are perishing* (2 Corinthians 2:14-15 NIV).

When my ex-husband left me with my six-year-old and one-year-old boys, I was coaching a little league T-ball team. Eight years later, a man approached me whom I use to coach T-ball with during that time. He came up to me and asked me what was going on. I gave him an update about my law school, marriage, and ministry. He looked at me and with emotion said, "Robin, you deserve it." I could see that this man was choked up. It moved me, seeing this take place.

MY PICTURE IS BEAUTIFUL

A few minutes later, a woman who had had a son on that same T-ball team came to me while I was volunteering at the soda cart. She asked me if I used to coach a little league T-ball team, to which I said yes. She then told me that her son had been a child on that team. She did not know how I had made it and was so impressed with how I was doing now. I testified about God's goodness, pulling me through such a hard time and bringing me to the other side of what appeared hopeless.

In our continued discussion, the woman went on and on about how her heart went out to me during the difficult times that she had seen me struggling through. When I continued to talk about what God had done with my life, she chose to stay and listen. Later on in the game, she came back again to talk with me. The very stench that sent people away before I came to the Savior was the same thing that was now drawing people to me. He had made me a sweet fragrance, and now others wanted to linger in the smell of it.

The incredible thing was that I did not even know that others were watching me go through the struggle during those years because I was in such a fog. Because they witnessed my struggle, they also witnessed my triumph in Christ Jesus. Your life is also available to be a sweet fragrance to others around you. All you need to do is give all your sins over to Jesus and rest in the fact that in Him you are *accepted!*

PRAYER FOR ACCEPTANCE IN CHRIST

Dear Lord Jesus, I confess that You are the Son of God and that You came to earth and died in order that I might live an eternity with You. I confess that I was a sinner, but now by faith I receive You as my Lord and Savior, thereby letting You take all of my sins away. I now take on Your righteousness and give You permission to take all of me—all of my heart—and use it for Your glory. In Jesus' name, I pray. Amen.

Sweet Fragrance

QUESTIONS:

1. In Section I, Chapter 1, where you wrote your story, how can any ungodly part of it now be used as a sweet fragrance for God?

2. Are you willing to see Jesus as the Lover of your soul and be undone before Him? If not, what is keeping you from seeing the truth? What Scriptures can you confess in Section IV for you to come into the truth?

3. What beautiful pictures are you coloring for Christ now?

4. What Scriptures can you confess in Section IV that will help increase your confidence in the fact that your life can now be a beautiful picture to the Lord? Is there anyone whom you have been feeling led to give your testimony to, because we overcome by the blood of the Lamb and the word of our testimony?

The Glory

SECTION FIVE

For the earth will be filled with the knowledge of the glory of the Lord, as the waters cover the sea (Habakkuk 2:14 NIV).

All I can say right now is that I am undone even thinking about doing this section regarding God's glory. First of all, there are complete books given over to studies regarding God's glory. Let me preface this section with the fact that there is no way to write only one section to cover everything considering God's glory. Therefore, if you have a deep hunger to learn more about the glory of God, I recommend getting all of Ruth Ward Heflin and David Herzog's books regarding the Glory, as I did years ago.

The Lord wanted me to do a section in this book in order to increase your hunger and expectancy for the glory of God in your life. Therefore, I am yielding myself to write about my personal experience with God's glory and what you can expect to see with the glory of God in your own life.

15

The Glory

I want to begin by laying a foundation of Scriptures that speak about God's glory. As we go through the rest of this section we will discuss where the glory of God goes—His mercy seat—and then how God wants to make you a walking mercy seat to receive the glory of God. Next, we will discuss the process of refinement whereby God makes us that glorious vessel of mercy. Finally we'll look at what you can expect from the glory of God in your own life. How will it look when God's glory is displayed in your life? Well, sisters, that is the task the Holy Spirit has laid out for this section, so buckle your seatbelts and let's get started. It is my hope that by the time you finish, you will have an understanding of God's glory.

GOD'S GLORY

The Hebrew word used for glory is *kâbôd,* which means "weight" in a figurative sense of the splendor or copiousness of God.[1] God's glory has a weight to it—heaviness. God's glory is tangible when it interfaces with our lives. It can look like many different things, and we will discuss that later. However, here I want to cover with you how the glory of God looked like in the Bible and how it looks throughout the present day.

Keep in mind that when God created Adam and Eve they walked every day in the glory of God (see Genesis 3:8-10). They walked in His presence. Therefore, when God first created man in His image, He created us for the glory. We see this as well in Jesus, who walked the earth and had the tangible display of God's glory all throughout His life.

Jesus is our goal in achieving the fullness of God in our lives. He came to redeem us from an eternity in hell and bring us to the Father to have eternal life with God. Jesus came to bring much more than redemption from eternity in hell. Jesus came to bring us the glory of God and show us how to walk in the glory of God all the days of our lives.

In the Bible, God's glory is displayed many times over through His presence. When God is present His glory is with Him. You cannot separate the presence of God from His glory—it is impossible. In God's glory is the fullness of who He is. He is Faithful, Healer, Redeemer, Provider, Justifier, Sanctifier, Lover, Victor; He is everything of who He is! The best way to describe this is by going to the first place in the Bible where a man, Moses, asks God to show him His glory.

> *Then Moses said, "Now show me Your glory." And the Lord said, "I will cause all My goodness to pass in front of you, and I will proclaim My name, the Lord, in your presence. I will have mercy on whom I will have mercy, and I will have compassion on whom I will have compassion. But," He said, "you cannot see My face, for no one may see Me and live." Then the Lord said, "There is a place near Me where you may stand on a rock. When my glory passes by, I will put you in a cleft in the rock and cover you with My hand until I have passed by. Then I will remove My hand and you will see My back; but My face must not be seen" (Exodus 33:18-23 NIV).*

Moses was a man who hungered after a relationship with God. He had an encounter with God at a burning bush. There, he received a commissioning from the Lord to bring His people out of Egypt, where they had been in bondage for over four hundred years. In Exodus 3, the burning bush was the first tangible encounter Moses had with God's glory. It was such a great presence of God that Moses could not step on the land with his shoes because it was holy ground. He even hid his face from God out of fear.

In the second book of this series, dealing with God's daughters being *Princess Warriors*, there is a section on the fear of the Lord which is important, because where God's glory is, there is a great anointing of the fear of the Lord—reverence for God. The fear of the Lord is seen in the encounter Moses had with God at the burning bush, because he hid his face from God, afraid to look at Him.

Let's fast-forward now from the burning bush to this encounter where Moses asks to see God's glory. After Moses has brought the children of Israel out of Egypt and is alone with God, he has a moment where he asks God to show him His glory. God does not reply to Moses, "Sorry, I do not want to show you My glory." No, what God responds to Moses is:

> *I will cause all My goodness to pass in front of you, and I will proclaim My name, the Lord, in your presence. I will have mercy on whom I will have mercy, and I will have compassion on whom I will have compassion* (Exodus 33:19 NIV).

God was telling Moses that His glory contains all of His goodness and when it passed by, God would proclaim His name, the Lord, in Moses' presence. God's glory contains all of who He is! His name has many facets all throughout the Word. God does not have one name but many.

Some of God's Names are *El* ("God mighty and strong"), *El Shaddai* ("God all-sufficient"), *Jehovah Jireh* ("the Lord will provide"), *Jehovah Raphe* ("the Lord who heals"), *Jehovah-M'Kaddesh* ("the Lord who sanctifies"), *Jehovah Shalom* ("the Lord our peace"), and *Jehovah-Tsidkenu* ("the Lord our righteousness").[2] The list goes on and on with the different names of God. When God was going to allow His glory to pass by Moses, He was in essence allowing all of who He is to pass by. That is why He told Moses that He would have to hide him in the cleft of the rock and not allow him to see His face. Moses would not have been able to live.

The reason that Moses could not live in that level of glory is because it was a high level of glory. No one on earth could live in that level. Therefore, God's glory is the essence of who He is. It is all of God, His majesty, splendor, wonder, and awe. God's glory comes with His presence. That is what Moses was experiencing at the cleft of the rock.

THE TENT OF MEETING

Another area in the Bible where God shows His glory is when Aaron and Moses are in the Tent of Meeting.

> *Then the cloud covered the Tent of Meeting, and the glory of the Lord filled the tabernacle. Moses could not enter the Tent of Meeting because the cloud had settled upon it, and the glory of the Lord filled the tabernacle. In all the travels of the Israelites, whenever the cloud lifted from above the tabernacle, they would set out; but if the cloud did not lift, they did not set out—until the day it lifted. So the cloud of the Lord was over the tabernacle by day, and fire was in the cloud by night, in the sight of all the house of Israel during all their travels* (Exodus 40:34-38 NIV).

Here, the glory of God *"filled the tabernacle."* This demonstrates that the tangible presence of God can occupy and fill an area. The Tent of Meeting was so full of God's tangible glory that Moses could not enter. The Tent of Meeting, also known as the tabernacle, was where Aaron and his sons ministered to the Lord; it kept the Ark of the Covenant. This place was constantly filled with the glory of God. Protocol had to be followed when Aaron and his sons entered the dwelling place of God, so that they would not die. This is depicted in Leviticus 10 when Aaron's sons, Nadab and Abihu, died for offering unholy fire to the Lord. In addition, Aaron was commanded not to have any fermented drink or wine when entering the Tent of Meeting, lest he die.

It is necessary to mention all of this information regarding the glory of God, because when you get to a certain level of glory you need to understand the fear of the Lord so that you can walk in that level of glory and live. I have not been to this level of glory myself, but I have read about it in Mel Tari's book, *Like a Mighty Wind*. However, I *have* encountered a level of glory of God when some of His angels entered a meeting I was in with Paul Keith Davis and Bob Jones. The presence of God on them was so powerful and so high that I thought I was going to die. The *kâbôd*—weighty presence of God—was so strong in that meeting that I felt like Isaiah did—that I was a woman of unclean lips.

ISAIAH

Isaiah had a great encounter with God's glory that left him forever changed.

In the year that King Uzziah died, I saw the Lord seated on a throne, high and exalted, and the train of His robe filled the temple. Above Him were seraphs, each with six wings: With two wings they covered their faces, with two they covered their feet, and with two they were flying. And they were calling to one another: "Holy, holy, holy is the Lord Almighty; the whole earth is full of His glory." At the sound of their voices the doorposts and thresholds shook and the temple was filled with smoke (Isaiah 6:1-4 NIV).

The seraphs were flying and calling to one another, saying, *"Holy, holy, holy is the Lord Almighty; the whole earth is full of his glory."* They were not whispering but screaming so loud that the doorposts and thresholds shook at the sound of their voice. Now that is loud! At the brilliance of being around the Lord without even seeing Him, the seraphs were overwhelmed. Can you imagine being in the weighty glory of God, not even seeing it with your eyes but merely being in the presence of God? It is beyond my mind to even imagine such a thing.

Their exclamation was also that the earth was *full* of God's glory. I have pondered a time or two about the earth being full of the glory of God. Many times, I would think to myself, "Well, when is it that I am going to see God's glory in the earth?" I was expecting to see a visible opening in Heaven where one day God would pour it out.

I am already aware of the Scripture that Peter quotes about God pouring out His Spirit on all flesh, and believe me, I know that that time is already here (see Acts 2:17-21). I am talking about the visible glory of God. As I have grown deeper in my relationship with God, I have recognized that, when more of His glory is in me, I am able to see His glory already filling the earth realm. I have realized that my eyes have been veiled to what already exists. The glory of God is here, covering the earth. I just could not see it. The seraphs were exclaiming that the earth was full of the glory of God when Isaiah had his encounter. This happened during a time when Israel was rebelling against God. Isaiah 1 is full of the rebelliousness identified in God's people.

During a time when God's people were rebellious, Isaiah had an encounter with God that left him undone. He knew who he was in the midst of God's glory:

> *"Woe to me!" I cried. "I am ruined! For I am a man of unclean lips, and I live among a people of unclean lips, and my eyes have seen the King, the Lord Almighty." Then one of the seraphs flew to me with a live coal in his hand, which he had taken with tongs from the altar. With it he touched my mouth and said, "See, this has touched your lips; your guilt is taken away and your sin atoned for"* (Isaiah 6:5-7 NIV).

Isaiah was "ruined" because he had seen who he was in the midst of God's glory. However, the good news was that God did not want to leave Isaiah in a place of agony. Rather, He sent atonement for Isaiah through the coal from the altar that touched his mouth. Likewise, God wants to bring us higher in His glory, and we are allowed to stay there because Jesus has made atonement for our sins. Jesus has taken our guilt away. Because of the sacrifice of Jesus Christ for our sins, we are able to walk into levels of glory with Him. Hebrews 9 goes into detail about how Christ gave His life, being the High Priest who entered Heaven's Most Holy Place, and gave His own spotless blood as atonement for our sin.

I Can See Your Glory God!

As I mentioned earlier, I was initially unable to see God's glory covering the earth as the seraphs described. After I had an encounter with God, my eyes were opened to this glory. My *understanding* of the levels of glory of God came through learning about His glory from Ruth Ward Heflin and David Herzog. However, my ability to *see* the glory of God came through an encounter I had shortly after reading one of Rick Joyner's books, *The Call*.

In *The Call*, Rick Joyner describes an encounter he had with the Lord that forever changed him. He explains that the Lord told him:

> *"When you start to live by what you see with the eyes of your heart, you will walk with Me, and you will see My glory. The eyes of your heart are your window into this realm of the Spirit. Through the eyes of your heart, you may come to My Throne of Grace, at any time. If you will come to Me, I will be more real to you. I will also trust you with more power."*[3]

After Rick Joyner had encountered the Lord in such a way, everything in the earth appeared as beautiful.

When I had an encounter with God during my devotion time one morning, it was as if He peeled off the scales that had been on my eyes that kept me from seeing His glory. I was now able to look at everything around me and see clearly the glory of God. I had a great conversation with my husband shortly after this experience, and he appeared more profoundly glorious than I had ever seen him. Colors were deeper and more brilliant than before. I was filled with utter joy unspeakable and felt that I was on the clouds while all of this was going on. It was one of the most incredible experiences I had with the Lord and His glory.

The glory of God is the manifest tangible presence of God. As we see with Moses, God's goodness and all He is—identified in His names—encapsulate His glory. Therefore, when we ask God for His glory, we are asking for His presence. Having had a foretaste of God's glory keeps me hungry for more. I am not satisfied with the level of glory I have seen but instead long for an encounter such as the prophet Isaiah's. God knows how much of His glory you can handle, and He will not put on you more than you can bear. Therefore, ask Him for His glory!

The Glory

QUESTIONS:

1. What does Moses discover with God's glory?

2. What does Isaiah discover with God's glory?

ENDNOTES

1. *New Strong's Concise Dictionary of the Words in the Hebrew Bible, with Their Renderings in the King James Version* (Nashville: Thomas Nelson Publishers, Inc., 1995), p. 62, #3519.

2. Lambert Dolphin, "The Names of God," Lambert Dolphin's Library, Old Testament, http://ldolphin.org/Names.html (accessed January 2, 2010).

3. Rick Joyner, *The Call* (Minneapolis, MN: Morningstar Publications, 2006), 30.

16

Knowing the King of Glory

*It is the glory of God to conceal a matter; to search out a matter
is the glory of kings* (Proverbs 25:2 NIV).

I n seeking the glory of God, I have discovered there is one focus we are to
have, and that one focus is getting to know Him—Father, Son, and Holy
Spirit. As we get to know God, our hunger for the glory is going to be a
by-product of our relationship. We will hunger for more of His presence in
our lives.

For example, my husband and I met through the Internet in August 2001
and married in December, 2001. My husband lived in Connecticut and I
lived in Alabama at that time. We met on a dating Web site. During our first
communication, I never thought that our relationship would go beyond a
"pen pal" friendship.

However, we went from communicating via the dating Web site to
communicating via e-mail. Then, once we had communicated via e-mail

awhile, we started communicating over the telephone. After talking on the telephone awhile, we wanted a face-to-face encounter—we wanted each other's presence. The hunger level started when we first communicated via a Web site, and it kept rising to a more intimate communication as we knew more of the other person. Before we had ever met face to face, believe it or not, we had already set a wedding date. I fell in love with my husband before I met him. That love in me stirred at such a level that I had to have him near me. I wanted to see him, hug him, and yes, most definitely kiss him!

OTHER GLORY ENCOUNTERS

It is no different with the Lord. As we get to know Him, we want more than just a communication with Him. We want His presence, and why not have it? It is a natural out-flow of a love relationship. This is how we get hungry for God's glory. King David is a great depiction of this type of hunger for the glory of God. We see how King David describes the Lord as the King of Glory.

> *The earth is the Lord's, and everything in it, the world, and all who live in it; for He founded it upon the seas and established it upon the waters. Who may ascend the hill of the Lord? Who may stand in His holy place? He who has clean hands and a pure heart, who does not lift up his soul to an idol or swear by what is false. He will receive blessing from the Lord and vindication from God his Savior. Such is the generation of those who seek Him, who seek Your face, O God of Jacob. Selah. Lift up your heads, O you gates; be lifted up, you ancient doors, that the King of glory may come in. Who is this King of glory? The Lord strong and mighty, the Lord mighty in battle. Lift up your heads, O you gates; lift them up, you ancient doors, that the King of glory may come in. Who is He, this King of glory? The Lord Almighty—He is the King of glory. Selah* (Psalm 24:1-10 NIV).

King David identifies who will see the glory of God in verse 6: *"Such is the generation of those who seek Him, who seek Your face, O God of Jacob."* David is saying that those people who seek the face of God are those who are hungry for His glory. Then David starts describing the glory.[1] The word "heads" in Psalm 24:7-9 actually comes from the Hebrew word *rôʾsh*, meaning "to shake." "Gates" in the same verses comes from the Hebrew word *shaʾar* and means "opening," as in a city, door, gate, or port.[2] The "ancient doors" David is talking about here are the doors of eternity. David was exclaiming that God was coming in His glory—the doors of eternity would shake the earth.

This is the very encounter Isaiah experienced with God in Isaiah 6. Remember that when the seraphs exclaimed, *"Holy, holy, holy is the Lord Almighty; the whole earth is full of His glory,"* the doorposts and thresholds "shook" (Isaiah 6:3 NIV). Therefore, when God's glory enters in, it shakes things!

When God takes us from glory to glory things in our lives are going to be shaken. God's glory shakes things that are not of Him off of us. The Tent of Meeting and the temple where Isaiah encountered God were able to stand the glory of God because those buildings had been dedicated to the Lord. God gave detailed instructions on how to build the Tent of Meeting. The temple during Isaiah's time had been dedicated to the Lord. This temple was holy. Uzziah, the King of Judah during Isaiah's time, went to burn incense to the Lord out of protocol. It was the priests place to burn incense to the Lord, but out of pride Uzziah felt that he could burn incense to the Lord as well. The head priest and eighty other priests warned Uzziah not to burn the incense. When he refused to heed their warning he was struck with leprosy. This demonstrated that God's glory was in the temple.

Take Me to the Next Level of Glory

Our bodies are the temple of God. Jesus demonstrated this as He walked the earth. He was angered by those merchandising and selling in the house of God, and the Jews confronted Him afterward, demanding a sign of His authority to do those things. Jesus makes a statement:

> *Jesus answered them, "Destroy this temple, and I will raise it again in three days." The Jews replied, "It has taken forty-six*

years to build this temple, and you are going to raise it in three days?" But the temple He had spoken of was His body. After He was raised from the dead, His disciples recalled what He had said. Then they believed the Scripture and the words that Jesus had spoken (John 2:19-22 NIV).

Jesus was not speaking of the temple building but rather of His own body. In the same manner that Jesus spoke of His body being the temple, Paul in First Corinthians spoke of us being the temple of the Holy Spirit.

Do you not know that your body is a temple of the Holy Spirit, who is in you, whom you have received from God? You are not your own (1 Corinthians 6:19 NIV).

The Holy Spirit comes to dwell in us just as God's glory dwelt in the temple and Tent of Meeting.

SHOW ME YOUR GLORY

There are different levels of glory, and we see this depicted in Second Corinthians 3:18 where God's Word says that He takes us from *"glory to glory."* This indicates that there are different levels of God's glory. Moses had already been in many levels of God's glory before He asked God to show him His glory. The reason Moses asked to see the glory of God was because he had reached an intimate relationship with God.

Our intimate relationship with God gets us to hunger for His glory. When we are at one level of glory our hunger gets us to crave for the next level of glory. As we are going from glory to glory, we are being transformed more into the image of Christ. We are experiencing more of God's presence, and it changes us. Therefore, when we ask for God's glory we are asking Him to change us. As Chuck Pierce so brilliantly put it in a conference I attended, "God changes not, so we have to change a whole lot." There is so much truth in this statement. God's Word states that He does not change (see James 1:17). Paul explains the process whereby we change.

Now the Lord is the Spirit, and where the Spirit of the Lord is, there is liberty (emancipation from bondage, freedom). And all of us, as with unveiled face, [because we] continued to behold [in the Word of God] as in a mirror the glory of the Lord, are constantly being transfigured into His very own image in ever increasing splendor and from one degree of glory to another; [for this comes] from the Lord [Who is] the Spirit (2 Corinthians 3:17-18 AMP).

The Scripture states that as we behold *"the glory of the Lord"* we are being *transfigured*, which means *changed*. God is constantly changing us into *His* image! And if you notice the next statement, it is with *"increasing splendor"* that He is changing us. This splendor is the very thing that we discussed earlier under the Hebrew word for glory—*kâbôd*. God is raising us up with Him in His own glory. Hallelujah! I don't know if that makes you happy, but it makes me want to shout for joy!

We who are the temple of the Holy Spirit are being changed! We are being changed into the splendor of God's glory! Not only on one level of glory but into levels of glory—from glory to glory to glory to glory! We are being changed into the very image of the Lord! Wow! That is such an awesome thing to behold. The evidence of this is so true when I look back over my life. I use to be a drunken, fornicating, bound-up woman. As a result of God's glory I have been set free from those bondages. As His glory has increased in me (my temple) those things which once held me captive have loosed me.

The Glory to Glory Sisterhood

The same is true for you. God is going to take you right where you are and move you to the next level of glory in Him. As you move from glory to glory with God, your testimony will help set other women free from bondage, too. I got free from my old lifestyle, and now I go preach in rehabilitation centers to former female inmates. The anointing of God in my life (His glory in my temple) is strong enough to free the captives who are in bondage to those very same things I once was. As I stated earlier, I had been in bondage to alcoholism. In breaking free of that stronghold I wrestled for my deliverance from it. I constantly declared that I was not an alcoholic but rather that I had the mind of Christ and am the righteousness of Christ Jesus. I continued to declare that over myself and broke the power of the devil off of my life in that area. As a result, when I have prayed with other people who have an addiction to alcohol or even pray for them in my prayer closet, I have seen them get released from that bondage.

God is looking for a company of women who will allow Him to take them from glory to glory. Will you be in this company of women? Will you be in the Glory to Glory Sisterhood?

In the next section we are going to cover how God changes us and what it feels like as we go from glory to glory. It is a beautiful yet painful process. The pain is eased a lot by God's goodness and His grace. The pain we experience is a dying to our flesh nature and walking in the Spirit. In order to get to the place where we are a temple for His glory, we have to become mercy seats. In the next chapter we will learn what the mercy seat is and how we can become one.

Knowing the King of Glory

QUESTIONS:

1. What is our focus if we are to go after God's glory?

2. Can you look at things in your own life and see how far God has brought you? Can you see His glory? Ask God to open up your eyes to see His glory.

ENDNOTES

1. *New Strong's Concise Dictionary of the Words in the Hebrew Bible, with Their Renderings in the King James Version* (Nashville: Thomas Nelson Publishers, Inc., 1995), p. 129, #7218.

2. Ibid., p. 146, #8179.

c h a p t e r

17

God's Mercy Seat

Before moving forward, please pray Ephesians 1:17-18 with me out loud, personalizing the verse with the words in parenthesis.

I keep asking that the God of our Lord Jesus Christ, the glorious Father, may give you (me) *the Spirit of wisdom and revelation, so that you* (I) *may know him better. I pray also that the eyes of your* (my) *heart may be enlightened in order that you* (I) *may know the hope to which He has called you* (me), *the riches of His glorious inheritance in the saints* (Ephesians 1:17-18 NIV).

This is my favorite chapter in this entire book because I can reveal an encounter I had with God that gave me His strategy and His heart for His children. Two things happened in February of 2004 that revealed God's heart and strategy. The first was at a Bible study on a Saturday night. During worship, the Lord told me that He was going to give me a crown. I was excited and told Him I would receive it. Realize that I am not talking about a crown in the physical world but in the spirit. Remember, we are body, soul, and spirit (see 1 Thess. 5:23). The crown the Lord gave me was a thin gold crown, and He told me that it was called the crown of holiness. I was so excited and told Him that I would receive it and thanked Him.

The second thing happened a couple of weeks after the crown of holiness, while I was interceding (praying) with the Lord in my home. As I was in the midst of worship, the presence of God was very strong. He told me to grab the horns of the altar and come to His mercy seat. (I will discuss this further in Chapter 18.) He told me to ask for His mercy and asked me if I knew what His mercy was.

I have discovered when God asks a question it is usually not because I know the answer. Rather, He is getting a revelation across to me. I responded, "No."

God told me, "There is power, there is miracle-working power, there is freedom in My mercy." Then He said, "Jesus, while on the earth, was My walking Mercy Seat." God gave me an invitation and told me that He was looking and His eyes were searching across the earth for mercy seats. He explained that when He pours out His glory, it is going to His mercy seats.

God showed me that we had not even scratched the surface of His mercy. It is as if we have scratched one little part of all the oceans in the world. His mercy is deeper and wider than we could ever imagine. At this revelation, I was blown away. I can understand how Jesus was a walking mercy seat, but for me to be one as well was intimidating. However, I know my God would not ask anything of me that was impossible.

Thus began my quest into God's mercy and the crown of holiness. I happened to be on the Internet, studying the priesthood of Moses' time. During my study, I came across a gold crown that Aaron wore that said, *"Holiness to the Lord."* God showed me that it was the crown of holiness that He had given me.

> *Then they made the plate of the holy crown of pure gold, and wrote on it an inscription like the engraving of a signet: Holiness to the Lord* (Exodus 39:30).

Aaron had to wear the crown of holiness when he entered the Most Holy Place—where God's glory rested—to make atonement for the sins of the people. God was showing me that He was calling me into a deeper level of holiness to encounter His glory, and this would occur as I yielded to the process of becoming a vessel of mercy.

GOD'S MERCY AND HIS GLORY

The mercy seat was the place where God purged sin, but it was also a place of communion between God and man.

God told Moses that He would appear in a cloud upon the Mercy Seat:

> *And the Lord said unto Moses, Speak unto Aaron thy brother, that he come not at all times into the holy place within the vail before the mercy seat, which is upon the ark; that he die not: for I will appear in the cloud upon the mercy seat* (Leviticus 16:2 KJV).

Here, God is identifying the place in which He will appear—upon the mercy seat. Remember, where God is, His glory is also.

> *You shall make a mercy seat of pure gold; two and a half cubits shall be its length and a cubit and a half its width. And you shall make two cherubim of gold; of hammered work you shall make them at the two ends of the mercy seat. Make one cherub at one end, and the other cherub at the other end; you shall make the cherubim at the two ends of it of one piece with the mercy seat. And the cherubim shall stretch out their wings above, covering the mercy seat with their wings, and they shall face one another; the faces of the cherubim shall be toward the mercy seat. You shall put the mercy seat on top of the ark, and in the ark you shall put the Testimony that I will give you. And there I will meet with you, and I will speak with you from above the mercy seat, from between the two cherubim which are on the ark of the Testimony, about*

everything which I will give you in commandment to the children of Israel (Exodus 25:17-22).

The mercy seat was the covering for the Ark of the Covenant and the place where God said that He would meet with Moses. The area in the Tent of Meeting where the Ark of the Covenant was placed was known as "The Holiest of All, The Most Holy Place."

When I read this Scripture it amazed me, and I was able to understand that God's mercy was a greater revelation than I had imagined. I knew that I had to study His mercy. God instructed me that His mercy is a demonstration of His love—an action. During this encounter with God in February, Valentine's Day happened to be around the corner. He showed me that, although I knew my husband Rich loved me, I still wanted to see a demonstration of his love. For example, I would love a demonstration of some fresh red roses, although I knew he already loved me. Likewise, God loves us, and He demonstrates His love by showing us mercy.

> *For you are a holy people to the Lord your God; the Lord your God has chosen you to be a people for Himself, a special treasure above all the peoples on the face of the earth. The Lord did not set His love on you nor choose you because you were more in number than any other people, for you were the least of all peoples; but because the Lord loves you, and because He would keep the oath which He swore to your fathers, the Lord has brought you out with a mighty hand, and redeemed you from the house of bondage, from the hand of Pharaoh king of Egypt. Therefore know that the Lord your God, He is God, the faithful God who keeps covenant and mercy for a thousand generations with those who love Him and keep His commandments* (Deuteronomy 7:6-9).

The Lord chose Israel because He loved them. He is a God that keeps covenant and *mercy* with His people. It was God's love for Israel that brought His mercy to them. Likewise, we are grafted into the family of God when we accept Jesus as our Lord and Savior, and we have His covenant of mercy, too (see Rom. 11:17).

THE ARK OF THE COVENANT

The Ark of the Covenant prophecies Jesus, and as we look at it we can see the elements that show who Jesus is. Inside the Ark of the Covenant were the Ten Commandments—the Law—and the Word of God states that Jesus came to fulfill the law.

> *Do not think that I came to destroy the Law or the Prophets. I did not come to destroy but to fulfill* (Matthew 5:17).

The Ark of the Covenant also held the manna in a gold jar:

> *Which had the golden altar of incense and the gold-covered Ark of the Covenant. This ark contained the gold jar of manna, Aaron's staff that had budded, and the stone tablets of the covenant* (Hebrews 9:4 NIV).

Jesus said that He is the bread of life:

> *Verily, verily, I say unto you, He that believeth on me hath everlasting life. I am that bread of life. Your fathers did eat manna in the wilderness, and are dead. This is the bread which cometh down from Heaven, that a man may eat thereof, and not die. I am the living bread which came down from Heaven: if any man eat of this bread, he shall live for ever: and the bread that I will give is my flesh, which I will give for the life of the world* (John 6:47-51 KJV).

Finally, the Ark of the Covenant held Aaron's rod that had bloomed (see Num. 17). The blooming of Aaron's rod signified the resurrection power of God. Christ displayed this resurrection power when He was raised from the dead. In Ephesians 1, Paul talks about our inheritance as a believer of Christ, and he also mentions the power of God that He worked in Christ when He raised Him from the dead. This power of God is resurrection power!

> *Therefore I also, after I heard of your faith in the Lord Jesus and your love for all the saints, do not cease to give thanks for you, making mention of you in my prayers: that the God of our Lord Jesus Christ, the Father of glory, may give to you the spirit of wisdom and revelation in the knowledge of Him, the eyes of your understanding being enlightened; that you may know what is the hope of His calling, what are the riches of the glory of His inheritance in the saints, and what is the exceeding greatness of His power toward us who believe, according to the working of His mighty power which He worked in Christ when He raised Him from the dead and seated Him at His right hand in the heavenly places, far above all principality and power and might and dominion, and every name that is named, not only in this age but also in that which is to come. And He put all things under His feet, and gave Him to be head over all things to the church, which is His body, the fullness of Him who fills all in all* (Ephesians 1:15-23).

These same items that prophesy about Jesus and are contained in the Ark of the Covenant are also extended to us by the grace of God. God's Word tells us that the Law is fulfilled in us through Jesus Christ.

> *There is therefore now no condemnation to those who are in Christ Jesus, who do not walk according to the flesh, but according to the Spirit. For the law of the Spirit of life in Christ Jesus has made me free from the law of sin and death. For what the law could not do in that it was weak through the flesh, God did by sending His own Son in the likeness of sinful flesh, on account of sin: He condemned sin in the flesh, that the righteous requirement of the law might be fulfilled in us who do not walk according to the flesh but according to the Spirit. For those who live according to the flesh set their minds on the things of the flesh, but those who live according to the Spirit, the things of the Spirit* (Romans 8:1-5).

The word of God goes on to tell us that we fulfill the law through love.

> *The commandments, "Do not commit adultery," "Do not murder," "Do not steal," "Do not covet," and whatever other commandment there may be, are summed up in this one rule: "Love your neighbor as yourself." Love does no harm to its neighbor. Therefore love is the fulfillment of the law* (Romans 13:9-10 NIV).

The manna that is in the Ark of the Covenant depicts Jesus as the Bread of Life. Paul explains that we partake of Jesus, the Bread of Life, and are a part of the same loaf.

> *Therefore, my dear friends, flee from idolatry. I speak to sensible people; judge for yourselves what I say. Is not the cup of thanksgiving for which we give thanks a participation in the blood of Christ? And is not the bread that we break a participation in the body of Christ? Because there is one loaf, we, who are many, are one body, for we all partake of the one loaf* (1 Corinthians 10:14-17 NIV).

Finally, Paul discusses us being resurrected with Christ.

> *In Him you were also circumcised, in the putting off of the sinful nature, not with a circumcision done by the hands of men but with the circumcision done by Christ, having been buried with Him in baptism and raised with Him through your faith in the power of God, who raised Him from the dead* (Colossians 2:11-12 NIV).

THE MERCY SEAT

Now that we have reviewed the Ark of the Covenant and how it prophesied Jesus, as well as how we also have the same fulfillment of the law through our love, are a part of the same loaf of bread that Jesus is, and are raised up with Christ, we can see how God is forming us into the image of Christ. The final thing I want to get to in this chapter is the mercy seat. The Ark of the Covenant contained the three items mentioned, but the Mercy Seat was the covering for the Ark of the Covenant.

The mercy seat, as discussed earlier, is where God told Moses that He would meet with him. Also, for the atonement of sins, the mercy seat had to have blood sprinkled on it. Likewise, Jesus gave His life as atonement for our sins. This was the greatest demonstration of mercy. The Mercy Seat prophesied Jesus from the moment it was designed and created by God.

All throughout Scripture, we see that where Jesus walked the mercy of God was present.

> *When Jesus departed from there, two blind men followed Him, crying out and saying, "Son of David, have mercy on us!" And when He had come into the house, the blind men came to Him. And Jesus said to them, "Do you believe that I am able to do this?" They said to Him, "Yes, Lord." Then He touched their eyes, saying, "According to your faith let it be to you." And their eyes were opened...* (Matthew 9:27-30).

> *And behold, a woman of Canaan came from that region and cried out to Him, saying, "Have mercy on me, O Lord, Son of David! My daughter is severely demon-possessed"* (Matthew 15:22).

> *And when they had come to the multitude, a man came to Him, kneeling down to Him and saying, "Lord, have mercy on my son, for he is an epileptic and suffers severely; for he often falls into the fire and often into the water. So I brought him to Your disciples, but they could not cure him"* (Matthew 17:14-16).

Jesus gives us a parable in Luke that demonstrates mercy on others and tells us to do likewise.

> *Then Jesus answered and said: "A certain man went down from Jerusalem to Jericho, and fell among thieves, who stripped him*

of his clothing, wounded him, and departed, leaving him half dead. Now by chance a certain priest came down that road. And when he saw him, he passed by on the other side. Likewise a Levite, when he arrived at the place, came and looked, and passed by on the other side. But a certain Samaritan, as he journeyed, came where he was. And when he saw him, he had compassion. So he went to him and bandaged his wounds, pouring on oil and wine; and he set him on his own animal, brought him to an inn, and took care of him. On the next day, when he departed, he took out two denarii, gave them to the innkeeper, and said to him, 'Take care of him; and whatever more you spend, when I come again, I will repay you.' So which of these three do you think was neighbor to him who fell among the thieves?" And he said, "He who showed mercy on him." Then Jesus said to him, "Go and do likewise" (Luke 10:30-37).

Jesus, who was the image of His Father, God, showed great mercy and told us to *"go and do likewise."* He extended an invitation for us to be a mercy seat for God, too. In the next chapter we will discuss further how we are invited to follow Jesus' example.

MERCY AND THE GLORY

Where God's mercy is, God's glory is, too. These two aspects connect because God communed with Moses over the mercy seat. Since God's presence was there, His glory was with Him. Moreover, when Moses asked God to show him His glory, God only allowed him to look at His back side, because no man could see the face of God and live. The glory of God's face is at such levels that people cannot even live. We see in Psalms that *"mercy and truth"* go before God's face. Since the glory of God is at such a high degree in His face and mercy and truth go before Him, then obviously mercy ushers in God's glory.

Righteousness and justice are the foundation of Your throne; mercy and truth go before Your face (Psalm 89:14).

Imagine a king or queen entering a room. They have ushers that go in before them. The ushers are a precursor to the entrance of the king and queen. God's mercy is a precursor of His glory, which is soon to manifest.

God's glory is also seen in the face of Jesus:

> *For it is the God who commanded light to shine out of darkness, who has shone in our hearts to give the light of the knowledge of the glory of God in the face of Jesus Christ* (2 Corinthians 4:6).

The Bible also states that God's glory was on Moses' face:

> *But if the ministry of death, written and engraved on stones, was glorious, so that the children of Israel could not look steadily at the face of Moses because of the glory of his countenance, which glory was passing away* (2 Corinthians 3:7).

As God tells us that He is going to take us from *"glory to glory,"* He tells us that we will have unveiled faces. The unveiled face is an indicator of the glory of God that will be seen upon us:

> *But we all, with unveiled face, beholding as in a mirror the glory of the Lord, are being transformed into the same image from glory to glory, just as by the Spirit of the Lord* (2 Corinthians 3:18).

To summarize, here we can see that God's glory is present with His mercy. God demonstrates to us how Jesus, the Son of God, was a walking mercy seat, providing mercy to those who put a demand on it. Likewise, Jesus tells us to pick up our cross and follow Him (see Luke 9:23-24). We are to follow His example of being a mercy seat to others on the earth. We are to show others the glory of God. In the next section we will look how we become vessels of mercy upon which God wants to pour out His glory. In being one of these vessels of mercy, there is a process of preparation.

God's Mercy Seat

QUESTIONS:

1. Where did God meet with Moses?

2. What did the Ark of the Covenant contain inside of it?

3. How are the elements that are inside the Ark of the Covenant demonstrated in Christ?

4. How are the elements that are inside the Ark of the Covenant demonstrated in us?

5. Where was the mercy seat?

6. What was the mercy seat used for and how is it similar to Jesus?

7. Where did Jesus command us to go and show mercy to others?

18

Romans 9:23 Vessel of Mercy

VESSELS OF MERCY CREATED
TO RECEIVE GOD'S GLORY

In asking me if I wanted to be a walking mercy seat, God showed me Romans 9:23.

> *That He might make known the riches of His glory on the vessels of mercy, which He had prepared beforehand for glory* (Romans 9:23).

When I came across this verse in Scripture I was so blown away, because it confirmed God's awesome request to me. I immediately yielded myself to God and asked Him to do whatever was necessary to make me a vessel of mercy that would *"make known the riches of His glory."* This invitation is not only for me, but for others who hunger to become a vessel of mercy as well.

This invitation humbled me and overwhelmed me at the same time; I could not speak or describe the overwhelming emotions I was experiencing. I was excited, elated, nervous, and uncertain. You name it, and chances are that I felt it. In starting me on the quest to become a vessel of mercy, God reminded me how I had "grabbed the horns of the altar" in my intercession with Him. I remembered doing so and had seen in the Bible that the altar at the Tent of Meeting had horns that were a part of the altar. The Lord also showed me that when there was a man in the Bible in need of mercy, he ran to the altar and grabbed hold of its horns.

> *Now Adonijah was afraid of Solomon; so he arose, and went and took hold of the horns of the altar. And it was told Solomon, saying, "Indeed Adonijah is afraid of King Solomon; for look, he has taken hold of the horns of the altar, saying, 'Let King Solomon swear to me today that he will not put his servant to death with the sword.'" Then Solomon said, "If he proves himself a worthy man, not one hair of him shall fall to the earth; but if wickedness is found in him, he shall die." So King Solomon sent them to bring him down from the altar. And he came and fell down before King Solomon; and Solomon said to him, "Go to your house" (1 Kings 1:50-53).*

Adonijah had done something that deserved death. He had taken the title of king in his own hands and held his own ceremony. However, it was Solomon who was to become king, and when the grievous act was brought to light, Adonijah feared that he would surely die. As a result, he ran to the altar and grabbed the horns, asking that King Solomon swear that he would not kill him. This Scripture paints a perfect picture of God's throne of grace that we are to go to in order to obtain mercy.

Hebrews 4 is one of my favorite chapters because it talks about the rest of God, the sword of the Lord, and God's throne of grace.

> *Seeing then that we have a great High Priest who has passed through the heavens, Jesus the Son of God, let us hold fast*

our confession. For we do not have a High Priest who cannot sympathize with our weaknesses, but was in all points tempted as we are, yet without sin. Let us therefore come boldly to the throne of grace, that we may obtain mercy and find grace to help in time of need (Hebrews 4:14-16).

Here God tells us to come *boldly* to His throne of grace so that we may obtain mercy. Adonijah boldly went to the altar to grab the horns when he needed mercy, and this is a demonstration of what we are to do. We are to boldly come to God and obtain mercy. The Scripture does not say *ask* for mercy but *obtain* mercy. The reason Adonijah obtained mercy from Solomon was because he refused to let go of the altar unless Solomon made a promise to him. We have to be consistent in coming to God's throne of grace to obtain mercy.

Since I was preparing to be a vessel of mercy, I had to learn to obtain mercy. The word of God states, *"Blessed are the merciful, for they shall obtain mercy"* (Matt. 5:7). The way I obtained mercy was by being merciful. As my logic kicked in regarding the mercy of God and how I would obtain it, I started to get nervous. I could foresee that I would be placed in a lot of circumstances where I would have to give mercy to others beyond myself. This did not make me jump up and down for joy initially.

PAIN AND BEAUTY

As I mentioned earlier, becoming a mercy vessel is both beautiful and painful. The best analogy of such an experience is when a pregnant mother gets ready to deliver a baby. My first son, Christopher, was born in 1991, and things were different from the way they are today. The preparations doctors made were more laborious than now. When I was ready to deliver Christopher, although it was a beautiful time, pain coincided with the beauty. First, I had to have an enema given to me by a nurse, and it was not at all like the ones you get at home. Believe me, it was a very uncomfortable procedure. Then, I was in labor for 36 hours. This was painful beyond description, until I was allowed to get an epidural that relieved the pain surges. Christopher was 9 pounds, 8 ounces, and since no one knew this, I had to struggle with two nurses trying to push down on my huge belly.

Finally, I had Christopher in my arms. I was so overwhelmed by this awesome miracle of God that I was holding. Having him at last totally nullified the pain that I had to go through in delivery. It was a painful process, but the beauty of the result far outweighed the pain.

The process God uses to transform us into vessels of mercy is painful for us, pressing in our soul at every turn. However, the outcome of His work in us is so beautiful that all of the pain we go through is nullified.

How to Become a Vessel of Mercy

When we submit to becoming a vessel of mercy, we are submitting to the refiner's fire and letting God shake everything in our lives. When we talk about the refiner's fire, we can see it in Scripture in God's refinement of the Levites.

> But who can endure the day of His coming? Who can stand when He appears? For He will be like a refiner's fire or a launderer's soap. He will sit as a refiner and purifier of silver; he will purify the Levites and refine them like gold and silver. Then the Lord will have men who will bring offerings in righteousness (Malachi 3:2-3 NIV).

The Levites were the priests of God. This is similar to the believers, because according to Scripture we are a royal priesthood:

> But you are a chosen people, a royal priesthood, a holy nation, a people belonging to God, that you may declare the praises of Him who called you out of darkness into His wonderful light (1 Peter 2:9 NIV).

God is going to purge us so that we will be purified. This purification of the refiner's fire comes through trials and tribulations.

Beloved, do not think it strange concerning the fiery trial which is to try you, as though some strange thing happened to you; but rejoice to the extent that you partake of Christ's sufferings, that when His glory is revealed, you may also be glad with exceeding joy (1 Peter 4:12-13).

If the trials that we are going through are purifying us, what exactly needs purification?

In this you greatly rejoice, though now for a little while, if need be, you have been grieved by various trials, that the genuineness of your faith, being much more precious than gold that perishes, though it is tested by fire, may be found to praise, honor, and glory at the revelation of Jesus Christ (1 Peter 1:6-7).

Our *faith!* It is the genuineness of our faith that is being tried in the fire.

If our faith is being tried in the fire of God, how does this look? If you know that God is a good God and that He wants to give you a hope and a future then the trial might look like this (see Jer. 29:11-13 NIV). You know in your heart that you are to be a schoolteacher; however, you are now 34 years old and have never gone to college. You find yourself grieved over the fact that you have never gone to get your degree in education. Knowing that God is a good God and wants to give you a hope, your faith will be tried if you step out and start working on your degree to become a teacher. It might be very difficult for you to get your degree, because you will have to juggle children and schedules. However, if God has told you to be a schoolteacher, then He has not changed His mind. If you want what God has for your life, you will have to go through the trials in order to get what God has promised you.

FIERY TRIALS

There are many other ways that trials can take form in our lives. Mine was when I went to get my law degree. I finally finished my degree in December 2008 at the age of 41. However, I started when I was 34, and I cannot begin to tell you the obstacles I experienced time and time again as I went after my law degree. At other times, my oldest son, Christopher, experienced many attacks of the enemy against his life. I had to stand on the promise that God did not bring death but life, and life abundantly through Jesus Christ.

No matter what my circumstances looked like, I had to pray and declare and believe the promises of God. My faith was not going to hook up with discouragement or disappointment. I did not have time for that; it was life and death with my oldest son. I continue time and time again to go through the refiner's fire with the testing of my faith.

Some women might experience relationship struggles where they have to walk through a divorce or separation that will try their faith. Usually, the enemy comes against women during divorce and separation to tell them they are no good, unlovable, and so on. However, God's Word says that we are *"accepted in the Beloved,"* that we are *"fearfully and wonderfully made"* (see Eph. 1:6; Ps. 139:14). We have to hook our faith into God's Word, not our circumstances or what people say about us.

> *Now faith is the substance of things hoped for, the evidence of things not seen. For by it the elders obtained a good testimony. By faith we understand that the worlds were framed by the word of God, so that the things which are seen were not made of things which are visible* (Hebrews 11:1-3).

> *But without faith it is impossible to please Him, for he who comes to God must believe that He is, and that He is a rewarder of those who diligently seek Him* (Hebrews 11:6).

It is our faith that pulls things from the invisible realm into the visible. That is why, in becoming a vessel of mercy, the trying of our faith is so important. God uses His priests to become a holy dwelling place, a tabernacle or temple for His Holy Spirit, to bring about His plans and purposes for the earth. If our faith is tainted, it would be like Aaron walking into the Most Holy Place after drinking wine. If you remember, Moses instructed Aaron that he was not to enter the Tent of Meeting if he had drunk wine or fermented drink, lest he die. God's glory was at such a high level that Aaron could not do anything that would profane God.

God wants to bring us into higher levels of glory, and He does this by purifying our faith. To God, our faith is as precious as gold. The Ark of the Covenant was made out of acacia wood and then overlaid with pure gold. We can be compared to the acacia wood, because many times throughout Scripture, God compares us to trees of righteousness. On top of our humanity, God sanctifies us and makes us useful for His work. Then He gives us the ability to have faith that His Word is true and that we can do what He says we can do and have what He says we can have.

Ultimately, God's plan is to allow us to bring His Kingdom into every area we go. Jesus taught on the Kingdom of God. He went about doing good works, healing the sick, casting out demons, and raising the dead. Jesus sent out His 12 disciples, commissioning them to do things that would require great faith.

> And as you go, preach, saying, "The Kingdom of Heaven is at hand." Heal the sick, cleanse the lepers, raise the dead, cast out demons. Freely you have received, freely give. Provide neither gold nor silver nor copper in your money belts (Matthew 10:7-9).

Jesus commissions us to do the same as the disciples. If we do not have the faith necessary for the glory of God to use us, we will fall short. I don't know about you, but I want to see people healed and set free from all types of bondages. It is my desire to raise people from the dead, too. However, if my faith is tainted and I cannot believe what God's Word says, then He will not be able to move in me to raise the dead. His Word teaches that I have the same power as Jesus Christ, and I must believe that through His power I can do everything He desires, even raise the dead.

When you submit yourself to becoming a vessel of mercy you are submitting to the process whereby your faith is tried. You will experience fiery trials, but do not think it strange—rejoice! Better than that, find some other sisters who are going through fiery trials (I call them "bonfires" for fun) and praise God for all the fires you are going through. Laugh with each other, pray for each other, hug each other, and cry with each other, but most of all *rejoice* with each other. For example, many of my sisters and I have gone through great financial losses in the past few years where we have had to depend on God for daily provision. There have been times that we have gotten together and fellowshiped and during our time together instead of griping and whining we got together and rejoiced at our trials and what they produced in each of us. The trials had made us stronger in the Lord and had grown our faith. We end up rolling on the floor laughing at the different things we have come through and just celebrating what God has brought us through.

SHAKE IT!

The second thing that happens when you want to become a vessel of mercy, is that you will be shaken like you have never been shaken before. I do not mean literally but spiritually. As I mentioned earlier, wherever the glory of God is in high measures, there is a literal shaking (see Ps. 24; Isa. 6). These biblical examples of shaking give us indications about the shaking that God will bring in our lives.

Haggai 2 is known as the chapter that prophesies the glory that is coming to God's house:

> For thus says the Lord of hosts: "Once more (it is a little while) I will shake Heaven and earth, the sea and dry land; and I will shake all nations, and they shall come to the Desire of All Nations, and I will fill this temple with glory," says the Lord of hosts. "The silver is Mine, and the gold is Mine," says the Lord of hosts. "The glory of this latter temple shall be greater than the former," says the Lord of hosts. "And in this place I will give peace," says the Lord of hosts" (Haggai 2:6-9).

God states that He is going to shake everything that can be shaken. The apostle Paul even discusses this prophecy in Hebrews as he encourages believers:

> See that you do not refuse Him who speaks. For if they did not escape who refused Him who spoke on earth, much more

shall we not escape if we turn away from Him who speaks from Heaven, whose voice then shook the earth; but now He has promised, saying, "Yet once more I shake not only the earth, but also Heaven." Now this, "Yet once more," indicates the removal of those things that are being shaken, as of things that are made, that the things which cannot be shaken may remain. Therefore, since we are receiving a Kingdom which cannot be shaken, let us have grace, by which we may serve God acceptably with reverence and godly fear. For our God is a consuming fire (Hebrews 12:25-29).

Here, Paul is describing the shaking that God is doing. It is a shaking of everything that is not of His Kingdom, because God's Kingdom cannot be shaken.

Shakings take various forms in our lives, too. It is different from the fiery trial, because the fiery trial is to test our faith. The refiner's fire purifies our faith in God's truth, and we trust only in Him. The shaking, on the other hand, is to get things off of us. We might have things in our lives that are not of God, and He has to remove them because they are not of His Kingdom. God separates the things of His Kingdom from those of the enemy's kingdom. Here, everything that is not of God will not remain.

Now, I will tell you that my husband, Rich, and I have gone through shakings as well, and all it has done is make our marriage more solid. Our marriage is rooted and grounded in Christ, and because of that foundation we have been able to stand during shakings. Our lives changed drastically when we gave all of ourselves to Christ in 2003. I asked God to make me humble, pull all my idols down, and give me prudence. We lost our beautiful two-story home, I lost my Lexus 300, and we lost all of our money and came into a season of extreme leanness.

During that season, God showed me that He wanted nothing to stand in front of Him; He wanted to be my all in all. God transformed my mind from a world system to a Kingdom system. Today, He is bringing in His blessings, but Rich and I had to go through several years of wilderness. We have more faith and agreement than we ever had before, and it would have never occurred had we not gone through the fire and the shaking of God.

New Beginning

Here's another aspect of shaking. If you are in relationships that are not rooted and grounded in God then those relationships will sever. However, if you have a marriage or children, you do not need to divorce them. You *never* divorce children. But, if your husband leaves, that is not something you can help. I have been in that circumstance. Although I was married for eight years and did not want a divorce, I had no say in the matter. The word of God is clear on the matter of marriage.

> *For the unbelieving husband is sanctified by the wife, and the unbelieving wife is sanctified by the husband; otherwise your children would be unclean, but now they are holy. But if the unbeliever departs, let him depart; a brother or a sister is not under bondage in such cases. But God has called us to peace. For how do you know, O wife, whether you will save your husband? Or how do you know, O husband, whether you will save your wife? (1 Corinthians 7:14-16)*

I thank God that He worked that divorce to my good, because I found out that I had made an idol out of my ex-husband, the doctor. My relationship with him was not rooted and grounded in Christ. After my ex-husband left me with my two boys, I had to have my mind realigned with God's Word. God commands in His Word not to put any other idols before Him, and I had (see Exod. 20:3). Amazingly, after being a single mother a few years, God brought me the most incredible man on the face of the earth. He brought me Rich, my "Italian Man." We married in December of 2001 and still feel like newlyweds.

I talk to women who have gone through divorces or broken relationships for a moment. You are not a defective part of the female gender. You are just as special, beautiful, and accepted by God as women who have never been divorced. Trust God that He will put everything concerning your destiny back on track, and *never* look back. When Lot and his wife were leaving Sodom and Gomorrah and they were instructed not to look back, Lot's wife did and became a pillar of salt (see Gen. 19:25-26).

Sometimes looking back at your past can keep you stuck and fill you with questions and regrets. God is not a God who would have you living a life of regret. He is a God who allows you to repent for what you have done, and He washes your sin away and gives you a new beginning. Do not feel condemned if your marriage did not work out, and do not think that you are less in the Kingdom of God because you have been divorced. Be *free!* (We will actually discuss this more in the next chapter.)

MIND OF CHRIST

All mind-sets that are not of God's Kingdom will be broken off a person during the shaking. For example, I had been having difficulty in a particular area with seeing myself as God sees me. I had been in bondage to the fear of man and was timid, I had low self-esteem, and I constantly flogged myself, thinking I was a bad person. Those mind-sets needed to be shaken off of me because they were not of God. I did have the Word of God in me during that season, but my eyes were still veiled as to my identity. Therefore, a season came along where there was so much shaking in my life that I felt as if I was in a dark pit and no one was there but Jesus and me. (I thank God that my husband, Rich, was very supportive during this time.) It felt as if the enemy was vomiting on me, and at every turn I was undergoing persecution for standing on my Christian beliefs.

God allowed the shaking so that I would "wake up" and see who I was in Christ Jesus. He wanted me to have the mind of Christ. Finally, the last straw came in another attack full of lies, attempting to knock me down. When that happened, suddenly those mind-sets that were not of God were shaken off of me, and I could see the truth about who I was. I felt like Superman coming out of that dark pit I had been in. My mind needed transformation by God's

Word, but some things also needed to be shaken off of me because they were hindering my ability to see who I was.

Move Forward!

Going through the fire and being shaken are preparation processes for God's glory in our lives. This is how God makes us vessels of mercy. We learn to have more compassion toward other people who have gone through similar trials and shakings. It helps us see God's mercy in our own lives, and it brings us up to a new level of seeing Him and His goodness, as Moses saw when he was hidden in the cleft of the rock.

I cannot describe how truly amazed I am when I look back over the past two decades of my life. I can see where I was and where God has brought me and what He has done to display His glory in my life. Often during the day or during worship, I am brought to a place of such gratitude that He could use me for His glory—someone so imperfect, who was on her way to the gutter. However, God saw the treasure in me even when others could not. He is truly the greatest treasure hunter there is.

> For you are a holy people to the Lord your God; the Lord your God has chosen you to be a people for Himself, a special treasure above all the peoples on the face of the earth. The Lord did not set His love on you nor choose you because you were more in number than any other people, for you were the least of all peoples (Deuteronomy 7:6-7).

God chose Israel to be His special treasure, not because they were the greatest, but because they were the least! Wow! That is exactly what God saw in me. I felt like the least, but now I feel like His special treasure.

Becoming a mercy vessel that will hold God's glory is a beautiful but painful process. It is the refiner's fire and the shaking of God. However, in the same way that a woman who delivers a baby does not remember the labor pain when she is holding the baby, the beauty God gives you through the process of becoming a mercy vessel will far outweigh the pain.

214

Mercy Vessels

QUESTIONS:

1. What does the fire of God do in our lives?

2. What does the shaking of God do in our lives?

3. Are there any areas in your life currently where you can see God's refining fire?

4. Are there any areas in your life currently where you can see God's shaking?

19

How Does the Glory Look in My Life?

All Your works shall praise You, O Lord, and Your saints shall bless You. They shall speak of the glory of Your Kingdom, and talk of Your power, to make known to the sons of men His mighty acts, and the glorious majesty of His Kingdom. Your Kingdom is an everlasting Kingdom, and Your dominion endures throughout all generations (Psalms 145:10-13).

When God's glory hits your life you will never be the same. You feel so grateful and blown away that all you'll be able to do is praise and bless His name. In addition, you will speak of the glory of His Kingdom, His power, His mighty acts, and the majesty of His Kingdom. His presence arrives in the areas of wealth, health, freedom, and power. There are many more areas that God's glory can manifest, but we'll discuss these specific areas.

When we discuss glory here, we are not talking about glorifying ourselves. Even Jesus did not glorify Himself.

> *Jesus replied, "If I glorify Myself, My glory means nothing. My Father, whom you claim as your God, is the one who glorifies Me* (John 8:54 NIV).

It is God's glory—His presence, which is all of who He is—being seen in us that makes people jealous for the Lord.

> *I say then, have they stumbled that they should fall? Certainly not! But through their fall, to provoke them to jealousy, salvation has come to the Gentiles* (Romans 11:11).

God's glory in our lives will make others hungry for it, and that is how it should be. I want God to be so glorious in my life that people will stop me and ask, "How did you become so blessed?" That will provide me opportunity to preach to them the glorious Kingdom of God! The other day, a lady in my office came up to me and said, "Robin I really enjoy being around you because you have this joy." Another lady in the office chimed in and said, "You have an awesome marriage with your husband; you are so blessed." This provided me an opportunity to testify of how God has blessed my life and my marriage. The two ladies sat in awe in seeing how God had brought me from a life of bondage to a place where I was prospering in my marriage, my relationships, provision, etc.

God wants us to prosper. *"Beloved, I pray that you may prosper in every way and that your body may keep well, even as I know your soul keeps well and prospers"* (3 John 2 AMP).

The prosperity that the Bible shares here is from the Greek word meaning to "succeed in reaching."[1] Many people look at prosperity as merely gaining wealth. Wealth can be a part of it but does not truly denote true prosperity. Some of the most prosperous people I know are missionaries overseas who do not have much financial resources. Moreover, being in social work I can tell you that most social workers are not rich financially, however they are very prosperous in the fact that they are succeeding in their desire to help others.

Prosperity here can be seen as us reaching the dreams and the goals that are inside of our heart, which include but are not limited to doing the work we want to do, having great relationships with our husbands and children, having great friendships with other women and contributing to Kingdom work that God has called you, too.

For example, Rich and I are by no means wealthy in the way people in our nation might view wealth. There are many more people much wealthier than us. However, we are pursuing our dreams together and love each other with the love of Christ. Moreover, we have a great relationship with my two boys, Christopher and Matthew. To top that off, we have very close familial ties with all of our relatives and have a church home with a group of people we love. We are prospering.

When God causes us to prosper, what actually happens is that our lives are lining up with God's will for our life and we have a peace that surpasses our understanding.

The word states, *"Lean on, trust in, and be confident in the Lord with all your heart and mind and do not rely on your own insight or understanding. In all your ways know, recognize and acknowledge Him, and he will direct and make straight and plain your paths"* (Proverbs 3:5-6 AMP).

Many times, Rich and I have actually gone to the food pantry when we did not have money. However, in the midst of that season when we did not have enough, we did not feel poor; we felt rich. The reason we felt rich is that God's glory in our life was causing us to prosper in our soul. The prosperity in our soul manifested in our lives with all of the things that were not of God were being burnt up in the midst of our trials and tribulations that it literally was setting us free from leaning on our own understanding. Instead, we determined to lean on God and have confidence in Him seeking for Him to direct our paths.

During this time, do you think that Rich and I were not succeeding in prosperity because we had to go to the food pantry? No, we were succeeding because the goal we had was to do the will of the Father! While pursuing God's will for our lives, Rich and I endured a season of leanness financially. This lean time did not mean we were not prosperous.

Therefore, the ultimate goal and manifestation of God's glory in our lives is the fact that we are prospering in Him. We are seeking after His will and are succeeding in reaching His goals for our lives. Jesus stated it best when He showed us how to pray the model prayer: *"Pray therefore, like this; Our Father Who is in heaven, hallowed (kept holy) be Your name. Your kingdom come, Your will be done on earth as it is in heaven"* (Matt. 6:9-10 AMP).

HEALING OF THE BODY

Bless the Lord, O my soul, and forget not all His benefits: who forgives all your iniquities, who heals all your diseases, who redeems your life from destruction, who crowns you with lovingkindness and tender mercies (Psalm 103:2-4).

God's desire is to *heal all diseases!* He does not want to leave one disease out. What's more, Jesus Christ bore our iniquities when He died for us.

But He was pierced for our transgressions, He was crushed for our iniquities; the punishment that brought us peace was upon Him, and by His wounds we are healed (Isaiah 53:5 NIV).

It is not only a few diseases that God wants to heal. God wants to heal all of our diseases—heart disease, cancer, AIDS, Parkinson's, Alzheimer's, blood diseases, bone diseases, skin diseases, cell diseases, organ diseases, *every disease!* When God's glory is present then diseases have to leave, because they cannot stay in the glory.

Jesus commanded us to go heal the sick, and since He is in us we are able to. Jesus, the express image of God's glory, demonstrated that where God's glory is, God's healing is, too.

...And great multitudes followed Him, and He healed them all (Matthew 12:15).

And the whole multitude sought to touch Him, for power went out from Him and healed them all (Luke 6:19).

Just as Jesus healed those who were physically sick, we must, too. When God's glory shows up in your life you will be able to pray for others and watch their healing manifest. Moreover, when the glory of God is at high levels in your life, your very presence will bring healing. Peter was a great example of both.

Now Peter and John went up together to the temple at the hour of prayer, the ninth hour. And a certain man lame from his mother's womb was carried, whom they laid daily at the gate of the temple which is called Beautiful, to ask alms from those who entered the temple; who, seeing Peter and John about to go into the temple, asked for alms. And fixing his eyes on him, with John, Peter said, "Look at us." So he gave them his attention, expecting to receive something from them. Then Peter said, "Silver and gold I do not have, but what I do have I give you: In the name of Jesus Christ of Nazareth, rise up and walk." And he took him by the right hand and lifted him up, and immediately his feet and ankle bones received strength. So he, leaping up, stood and walked and entered the temple with them—walking, leaping, and praising God. And all the people saw him walking and praising God. Then they knew that it was he who sat begging alms at the Beautiful Gate of the temple; and they were filled with wonder and amazement at what had happened to him (Acts 3:1-10).

In this example, Peter touched the man and lifted him and the healing was made manifest. As God's glory increased on Peter, he was able to walk down the street and his shadow healed people.

And through the hands of the apostles many signs and wonders were done among the people. And they were all with one accord in Solomon's Porch. Yet none of the rest dared join them, but the people esteemed them highly. And believers were increasingly added to the Lord, multitudes of both men and women, so that they brought the sick out into the streets and laid them on beds and couches, that at least the shadow of Peter passing by might fall on some of them. Also a multitude gathered from the surrounding cities to Jerusalem, bringing sick people and those who were tormented by unclean spirits, and they were all healed (Acts 5:12-16).

This is something that I desire. I desperately desire to be so full of the glory of God that merely walking by people would heal them. I am not there yet, but I have seen God heal people as I lay my hands on them and prayed for them. There was a woman with a huge goiter who received prayer one night; the very next day, she woke up and it was gone. I have felt bones popping into place while people were being prayed for. These occurrences have increased my faith, and I hunger for more of God's glory in my life in the area of healing. Reading John G. Lake's sermons also increased my faith for healing, because he was known for the healing rooms where the sick came to be prayed for and were healed.

HEALING OF BROKENNESS

There is not only physical healing when God's glory is manifested, but there is also healing for the brokenhearted. Many throughout the world are in need of healing for broken hearts. There are so many broken homes, broken children, and broken adults that it's like the poem "Humpty Dumpty." People whose lives have been broken to pieces need to be put back together again. That is what Jesus came to do.

The Spirit of the Lord God is upon Me, because the Lord has anointed Me to preach good tidings to the poor; He has sent Me to heal the brokenhearted... (Isaiah 61:1).

In the Book of Luke, Jesus read this Scripture when he took the scroll.

So He came to Nazareth, where He had been brought up. And as His custom was, He went into the synagogue on the Sabbath day, and stood up to read. And He was handed the book of the prophet Isaiah. And when He had opened the book,

He found the place where it was written: "The Spirit of the Lord is upon Me, because He has anointed Me to preach the gospel to the poor; He has sent Me to heal the brokenhearted, to proclaim liberty to the captives and recovery of sight to the blind, to set at liberty those who are oppressed; to proclaim the acceptable year of the Lord." Then He closed the book, and gave it back to the attendant and sat down. And the eyes of all who were in the synagogue were fixed on Him. And He began to say to them, "Today this Scripture is fulfilled in your hearing" (Luke 4:16-21).

What is a brokenhearted person? "Broken" means "something that is fragmented, ruptured, fractured."[2] Therefore, a brokenhearted person is someone who feels as though their soul has been ruptured into a million pieces. The soul consists of the mind, will, and emotions. When someone has become brokenhearted it's as if their soul is so fragmented or crushed that they cannot pull themselves back together again.

When my oldest son, Christopher, had a skateboard accident and landed on his arm he was carried by an ambulance to the emergency room. His arm was swollen and appeared so disjointed that I could not look at it. The doctor came in and told me that it could be one of two things. First, it could be dislocated. If that was the case, it would only take a couple of minutes to pop it back in and send him on his way. However, it could also be broken. If it were fragmented a lot, then the treatment would be much more involved, requiring more time to heal. Fortunately for us, it was only dislocated, and all they had to do was pop it back into joint and send him home.

Understanding the difference between a dislocation and an actual break in the arm made me realize something. A broken bone is much more serious than I had perceived, and it requires a length of time to heal once it is set in a cast. A broken bone occurs due to a trauma.

There are some traumas in our lives that can leave us so brokenhearted that it feels impossible to recover. I know, because I went through that when my ex-husband, the doctor, left me with my two boys. I truly knew that my heart was so fragmented and fractured that recovery didn't seem possible. Thank God for an encounter with Him that healed my broken heart.

As a result of my experience, God has opened doors for me to preach and minister to other brokenhearted women. Since His glory has increased in my life, I am able to speak to the brokenhearted women God sends me and see them healed! The most incredible blessing—and I give God all the glory for this—is that while I am standing there speaking the word of the Lord to them, they literally transform. Their faces look different right in front of my eyes. They end up having this awesome glow come over them, and it's as if God placed the oil of gladness on them (see Isa. 61:3).

Jesus expects us to do greater works than He did on the earth.

> *Most assuredly, I say to you, he who believes in Me, the works that I do he will do also; and greater works than these he will do, because I go to My Father. And whatever you ask in My name, that I will do, that the Father may be glorified in the Son. If you ask anything in My name, I will do it* (John 14:12-14).

We are going to do greater works because Jesus went to be with the Father. When we do greater works, asking for healing in Jesus' name, it glorifies God! Moreover, when we ask anything in His name, He will do it. Sisters, we have to go forward, believing that God will give us His glory, stepping out in the name of His Son Jesus Christ, and asking Him for healings.

FREEDOM

God wants to see people set free from any captivity they might be in. When someone is a captive they are basically a prisoner being held in confinement. The captivity that God is talking about means exile (see Isaiah 61:1). If a person is exiled, they are banished from their own country. When we come into the household of faith in Jesus Christ, what is our country and where is our citizenship? Our citizenship is in the Kingdom of Heaven! When we are an exile we feel as if we are far from the Kingdom of Heaven. In Heaven there are no depressions, mental torments, sleep disturbances, bad dreams, voices in our heads, bad thoughts, addictions to narcotics and alcohol, or eating disorders. In Heaven we are more than conquerors through Christ Jesus—we have the mind of Christ; we have joy unspeakable.

The enemy, satan, comes along with his demons to convince us that we are not from the Kingdom of Heaven. He gets us to accept depression, mental torment, sleep disturbance, and more. By accepting this stuff from the enemy, we are allowing ourselves to be pulled away from our country, the Kingdom of Heaven. As I have walked deeper with the Lord, I constantly read and profess Isaiah 61 over and over throughout my Christian walk. In the beginning of that chapter in Isaiah, the Word of God hits everything that could possibly be holding us back in our Christian walk. The enemy is holding one of these things captive as a prisoner.

> The Spirit of the Lord God is upon Me, because the Lord has anointed Me to preach good tidings to the poor; He has sent Me to heal the brokenhearted, to proclaim liberty to the captives, and the opening of the prison to those who are bound; to proclaim the acceptable year of the Lord, and the day of vengeance of our God; to comfort all who mourn (Isaiah 61:1-2).

What does this Scripture mean, "proclaiming liberty to the captives"? When we proclaim liberty we are speaking the word of God—His truth to those who have become captive. Captivity results from coming into agreement and accepting things that are from the enemy. When we are held captive or exiled away from our country, we are not walking in the divine Kingdom of Heaven—what Jesus died on the Cross to pay the price for. When Jesus died He brought us eternal life and salvation.

FREEDOM THROUGH OUR SALVATION

What is salvation? When God parted the Red Sea to allow His people safe passage to the other side and then drowned the Egyptian army, Moses sang a song to God. He sang of the salvation of his God.

> *The Lord is my strength and my song; He has become my salvation. He is my God, and I will praise Him...* (Exodus 15:2 NIV).

Salvation here is *yshuwah* (pronounced yesh-oo-aw), which means "deliverance, health, help, save, victory, prosperity and aid."[3] Moses was saying, "God, You are my help when I need it. God, You are the One who brings me victory. God, You are the One who heals me and prospers me. God you are *all that!*"

Moses knew that he needed God to deliver him from the enemy's plans. He also needed God to bring him into prosperity, to give him divine health, and aid him at every turn. God saved him from everything that would speak death and defeat. Webster's defines "saved" as "to deliver from sin, to rescue or deliver from danger or harm, to preserve or guard from injury, destruction, or loss."

Like Moses, we need God's salvation to keep us from destruction, attacks, danger, and harm. Moreover, we need His salvation to bring us into prosperity and health in our emotions, mind, and body. King David sings this as well:

> *The Lord is my light and my salvation—whom shall I fear? The Lord is the stronghold of my life—of whom shall I be afraid?* (Psalms 27:1 NIV)

With God's salvation there is *nothing* to fear—no man, no circumstance, no illness, no situation, no "thing." *Nothing.* When we have become captive to the enemy's schemes, plots, plans, assignments, or traps—including things like depression, mental torment, alcohol abuse, drug abuse, and eating disorders—then we are not appropriating the fullness of God's salvation for us!

When we are walking in the glory of God in our lives we are going to be free from the captivity that the enemy once held us in. We will have such boldness in what God has done for us that we will desire the same for others. As we proclaim the truth about the Word of God and the Kingdom of Heaven, the prison doors that once held others in captivity will open and they will come out. God's glory is going to show in us as we walk in great freedom and proclaim the liberty of the Kingdom of Heaven so that others will walk in freedom, as well. (In the second book of this series, *Princess Warriors*, I discuss spiritual warfare in further detail.)

POWER

Get ready, ladies, because you are totally going to love this part. Have you ever watched a movie with a strong heroine and felt something rising up in you, like a hunger for *power?* I hope so, because God has given us a hunger for power. Why is that? He is the God of power! His Spirit of Might in Isaiah 11:2 is seen all throughout the Bible and is demonstrated in great measure.

God states how powerful He will make Abraham.

> *Then the Lord said, "Shall I hide from Abraham what I am about to do? Abraham will surely become a great and powerful nation, and all nations on earth will be blessed through him* (Genesis 18:17-18 NIV).

King David proclaims the power God gives His people.

> *You are awesome, O God, in your sanctuary; the God of Israel gives power and strength to his people. Praise be to God!* (Psalms 68:35 NIV)

God desires to give His people power!

Where does this power of God's glory come from? Why, it is His Holy Spirit! Jesus talks about this power in the Book of Acts.

> *So when they met together, they asked Him, "Lord, are You at this time going to restore the kingdom to Israel?" He said to them: "It is not for you to know the times or dates the Father has set by His own authority. But you will receive power when the Holy Spirit comes on you; and you will be My witnesses in Jerusalem, and in all Judea and Samaria, and to the ends of the earth"* (Acts 1:6-8 NIV).

Jesus stated that Peter and the rest of those who tarried in the upper room would receive *power* when the Holy Spirit came on them. God's Holy Spirit is the glory of God! It is God's presence in us! When we walk in the power of the Holy Spirit we are walking in the glory of God.

Before I received the Holy Spirit, I constantly felt defeated in trying to live a life of victory and purity at every turn. However, after receiving the Holy Spirit, I was able to walk in great power, able to do things I could not do before. Temptations that had kept me in bondage before completely fell off of me and had no pull on me. My victim mentality completely broke off when I had the power of the Holy Spirit in me. As I walked in more power with the Holy Spirit, I hungered for more and more of a relationship with the Holy Spirit. I do have a relationship with God the Father, Jesus my Savior and King, and the Holy Spirit. I thank them individually and talk to them individually as I am in relationship with them. Without God's Holy Spirit we have no power.

Jesus said that this power would come upon those in the upper room. It is necessary to read the entire chapter of Acts 2, because it describes the experience of the 120 disciples in the upper room. After they were filled with the Holy Spirit, as Jesus had instructed them, they were able to be a witness to Him to the ends of the earth.

> When the day of Pentecost came, they were all together in one place. Suddenly a sound like the blowing of a violent wind came from Heaven and filled the whole house where they were sitting. They saw what seemed to be tongues of fire that separated and came to rest on each of them. All of them were filled with the Holy Spirit and began to speak in other tongues as the Spirit enabled them. Now there were staying in Jerusalem God-fearing Jews from every nation under Heaven. When they heard this sound, a crowd came together in bewilderment, because each one heard them speaking in his own language. Utterly amazed, they asked: "Are not all these men who are speaking Galileans? Then how is it that each of us hears them in his own native language? Parthians, Medes and Elamites; residents of Mesopotamia, Judea and Cappadocia, Pontus and Asia, Phrygia and Pamphylia,

Egypt and the parts of Libya near Cyrene; visitors from Rome (both Jews and converts to Judaism); Cretans and Arabs—we hear them declaring the wonders of God in our own tongues!" Amazed and perplexed, they asked one another, "What does this mean?" (Acts 2:1-12 NIV)

All of the God-fearing Jews from different nations who spoke different languages were able to hear their own native language, and they were perplexed. There is no way that different nations would be able to hear their own languages from these spirit-filled Christians without the power of God's Holy Spirit. By the time Peter got through preaching his first sermon to this huge crowd of people, 3,000 people had come to receive Jesus Christ as their Savior by the power of the Holy Spirit.

With many other words he warned them; and he pleaded with them, "Save yourselves from this corrupt generation." Those who accepted his message were baptized, and about three thousand were added to their number that day (Acts 2:40-41 NIV).

Wow! Now that is an altar call!

How would you like the ability to walk in such great power by God's Holy Spirit that you would be able to do the very same things Jesus did? Peter and the apostles followed after Jesus and walked in great power.

With great power the apostles continued to testify to the resurrection of the Lord Jesus, and much grace was upon them all (Acts 4:33 NIV).

This power that the apostles walked in empowered them to testify about Jesus, heal the sick, cleanse lepers, raise the dead, cast off demons, and much more. This was *great power!*

When we walk in the glory of God, the Holy Spirit is going to be so increased in us that we will walk in truth and clarity, knowing who we are in Christ. Christ in us is the *hope of glory!*

The mystery that has been kept hidden for ages and generations, but is now disclosed to the saints. To them God has chosen to make known among the Gentiles the glorious riches of this mystery, which is Christ in you, the hope of glory (Colossians 1:26-27 NIV).

When we have the Holy Spirit we have the glory of God. Jesus depicts this well in John. He told the disciples of His departure and said that He would not leave the disciples as orphans, but instead would send the Holy Spirit.

Now I am going to Him who sent Me, yet none of you asks Me, "Where are You going?" Because I have said these things, you are filled with grief. But I tell you the truth: It is for your good that I am going away. Unless I go away, the Counselor will not come to you; but if I go, I will send Him to you. When He comes, He will convict the world of guilt in regard to sin and righteousness and judgment: in regard to sin, because men do not believe in Me; in regard to righteousness, because I am going to the Father, where you can see Me no longer; and in regard to judgment, because the prince of this world now stands condemned. I have much more to say to you, more than you can now bear. But when He, the Spirit of truth, comes, He will guide you into all truth. He will not speak on His own; He will speak only what He hears, and He will tell you what is yet to come. He will bring glory to Me by taking from what is Mine and making it known to you. All that belongs to the Father is Mine. That is why I said the Spirit will take from what is Mine and make it known to you. In a little while you will see Me no more, and then after a little while you will see Me (John 16:5-16 NIV).

The Holy Spirit has told me so much that I cannot even begin to tell you all He has told me. He has told me when my own family was in danger and I should pray and call them. He has told me when others were battling things that could harm them. He has told me when circumstances and people were going to bring attacks. He has told me of the blessings of God coming my way. He has shown me when to speak the Word of God over a matter to bring forth great fruit and results. He has shown me so much! Without the Holy Spirit, I would be in the dark on everything!

RECEIVING POWER

How do you receive the Holy Spirit? You simply ask God to baptize you in the Holy Spirit; it is a free gift from Him. You have to be born again and receive Jesus as your Lord and Savior before being baptized with the Holy Spirit. Ask God for the baptism of the Holy Spirit, and He will gladly do it.

> *I baptize you with water for repentance. But after me will come one who is more powerful than I, whose sandals I am not fit to carry. He will baptize you with the Holy Spirit and with fire* (Matthew 3:11 NIV).

Jesus came to baptize us with the Holy Spirit. Paul dealt with people who had been baptized unto repentance but not with the Holy Spirit. He made sure that they received the baptism of the Holy Spirit.

> *Paul said, "John's baptism was a baptism of repentance. He told the people to believe in the One coming after him, that is, in Jesus." On hearing this, they were baptized into the name of the Lord Jesus. When Paul placed his hands on them, the Holy Spirit came on them, and they spoke in tongues and prophesied. There were about twelve men in all* (Acts 19:4-7 NIV).

Simply ask God the Father to give you the Holy Spirit and He will. Before asking for the Holy Spirit, say a prayer of repentance so that your heart is right with the Lord. I have a prayer below if you feel led to pray it. Know that when you pray this, every good gift comes from the Father of Lights (see James 1:17).

> *Ask and it will be given to you; seek and you will find; knock and the door will be opened to you. For everyone who asks receives; he who seeks finds; and to him who knocks, the door will be opened. Which of you, if his son asks for bread, will give*

him a stone? Or if he asks for a fish, will give him a snake? If you, then, though you are evil, know how to give good gifts to your children, how much more will your Father in Heaven give good gifts to those who ask Him! (Matthew 7:7-11 NIV)

You are asking God for the Holy Spirit, you are seeking God, and you are knocking on the door! Believe and receive!

Please go get some readings or materials on the Holy Spirit. David Yonngi Cho has an awesome book, *Holy Spirit My Senior Partner*. I recommend it.

When the glory of God manifests in your life you will be able to see wealth (prosperity), healings of body, healings from brokenheartedness, freedom, and power!

PRAYER

*Father God, I thank You for all of Your goodness. I recognize that You are a Holy God, and I thank You for the gift of salvation through Your Son Jesus Christ. I repent of any sins that I have committed that are not under the blood of Jesus Christ. I ask that You cleanse me of all of my sins, and I thank You for removing my sins and washing me white as snow. Now, God, as an act of faith, I believe Your Word that says that Jesus came to baptize with the Holy Spirit. In faith, knowing that You will not give me anything bad if I ask for this gift of the Holy Spirit, I ask you **now** to baptize me in the Holy Spirit in Jesus' name.*

How Does the Glory Look?

QUESTIONS:

1. What does God's Word say about wealth?

2. What does God's Word say about healing?

3. What does God's Word say about freedom?

4. What does God's Word say about power?

ENDNOTES

1. *Webster's New World Dictionary of the American Language* 2nd College Edition (New York: Prentice Hall Press, 1986).

2. http://dictionary.reference.com/browse/broken.

3. *New Strong's Concise Dictionary of the Words in the Hebrew Bible, with their Renderings in the King James Version* (Nashville: Thomas Nelson Publishers, Inc., 1995), p. 61, #3444.

The Symbols of the
Glory to Glory Sisterhood

When God gave me the Glory to Glory Sisterhood as His sorority, "God's Sorority," I told Him that usually other sororities have symbols. I asked if we could have some for the Glory to Glory Sisterhood, or GGS. He gave me confirmation that it was fine with Him, and so I began to seek out what might best typify this sorority. As I was on a search, the Holy Spirit brought to my mind the crown and the six-point star. When I studied what the Scripture says about these things, I knew that the crown and star were the perfect symbols for the sisterhood. There are shirts and jewelry that are available for the sisterhood with the purpose of letting us connect with our sisters—whether we meet them walking down the street or in different areas across the world. When we see them wearing something of the sisterhood, we can connect with them.

God's Sorority brings women into unity, helping us see each other through the eyes of Christ. If I am going across the country and need someone to hook up in agreement with a prayer and I see one of my sisters, I will go to her and ask her to pray with me. If you see other sisters wearing apparel or jewelry with the symbols of the sisterhood, know that you have someone to pray with you.

THE CROWN

Many places throughout Scripture, the Lord speaks about a crown for His people. In the Book of Revelation, Jesus tells us that we will gain the crown of life if we overcome:

> *Do not be afraid of what you are about to suffer. I tell you, the devil will put some of you in prison to test you, and you will suffer persecution for ten days. Be faithful, even to the point of death, and I will give you the crown of life* (Revelation 2:10 NIV).

He reminds us:

> *I am coming soon. Hold on to what you have, so that no one will take your crown* (Revelation 3:11 NIV).

I want to end with the crown of glory that is found in Proverbs. Remember how I discussed the Spirit of Wisdom earlier in regards to wealth. Well, this same Spirit of God also gives us a crown of glory, which I especially love since we are the Glory to Glory Sisterhood!

> *"Exalt her, and she will promote you; she will bring you honor, when you embrace her. She will place on your head an ornament of grace; **a crown of glory** she will deliver to you." Hear, my son, and receive my sayings, and the years of your life will be many* (Proverbs 4:8-10).

I definitely want this crown of glory.

STAR

The star that is used as a symbol for the Glory to Glory Sisterhood is the six-point Star of David. Jesus is the bright Morning Star.

I, Jesus, have sent My angel to give you this testimony for the churches. I am the Root and the Offspring of David, and the bright Morning Star (Revelation 22:16 NIV).

Wow, that's holy! It just hit me. I pray to God that the revelation of Jesus being the bright Morning Star is opened up to you in Jesus' name!

Finally, in Scripture we are depicted as those who will shine like the stars.

Those who are wise will shine like the brightness of the heavens, and those who lead many to righteousness, like the stars for ever and ever. But you, Daniel, close up and seal the words of the scroll until the time of the end. Many will go here and there to increase knowledge (Daniel 12:3-4 NIV).

I don't know about you, but I truly want to shine like the stars forever and ever. I want to lead many to righteousness! I cannot help it, because the meaning of my name is "shining fame."

I pray that God fills you to overflowing with His glory, and you come into a radical relationship with King Jesus like never before. I pray God puts a fiery seal upon your heart and a seal upon your arm, and you will have the love for King Jesus that God has. (See the Song of Solomon 8:6-7.) I pray that the Holy Spirit will bring you into the fullness of God's plans and purposes for your life. I pray that you will have a Spirit of Wisdom so you may know Him better. I pray that the eyes of your heart will be enlightened to know the hope to which He has called you to—the riches of His glorious inheritance for all the saints and His awesome great power (see Eph. 1:17-19). In Jesus' name! Amen!

Author's Ministries

The Glory to Glory Sisterhood

Contact information: http://glorytoglorysisterhood.com

e-mail: robin@glorytoglorysisterhood.com

Princess Warriors

Contact Information: http://glorytoglorysisterhood.com

e-mail: robin@glorytoglorysisterhood.com

22 IS 22

Contact Information: http://22is22.com

e-mail: robinkg@22is22.com

Robin Kirby-Gatto's Other Books

Princess Warriors

At His Feet

Destiny